What Others Are Saying About This Book

"Growing up, my family made a special effort to celebrate the Christmas season together. When I started my own family, I looked forward to shaping my own Advent traditions. Borrowing from the ideas that John used with his family meant I didn't have to reinvent the wheel. When my children were babies and toddlers I was eager to help John make his book more age-appropriate, so we could start using it right away. As they've grown and matured, we've continued to use the book. We have enjoyed transitioning to the more in-depth questions and meanings from the same Advent themes we have used many years every December."

–Emily Bosh

"This Advent book has prompted us to set aside time as a family in the weeks leading up to Christmas. The book has numerous ideas to choose from each week to focus family time on worship and prayer, creating traditions that keep our focus on Christ. We highly recommend this resource for families with kids of all ages!"

–Damon and Polly DeLapp

"This Advent book is a great resource for helping families and church communities connect through the celebration of Advent. Our church used it as the basis for an all-ages Advent program, where we invited everyone to come together to remember the importance of the season. Using this book as a resource, we were able to include activities that were engaging for children, parents, and grandparents! What a wonderful way to connect within the generations of our church community."

–Kendra Paker

1

Thoughts from the Lewis Kids when in High School

The "Holy Family" in 1998 at the Lewis household, with Jonathan as Joseph, Ellie as Mary, and Rachel as the Baby Jesus.

"Our family Advent experience always prepared my mind and heart for the Christmas season, and the fact that Jesus was born for each of us."

– Jonathan

"Our family celebrated Advent together as long as I can remember. I love all the activities we did as a family, from acting out the Adam and Eve story to watching Charlie Brown's classic video. The Christmas season would have been very different without the Advent traditions we did together."

– Ellie

"Many of my most treasured Christmas memories had something do with this Advent book. For a kid, what could be better than getting to turn the light of the world on and off when I plugged in the Christmas tree? Our family Advent experience never failed to remind me of what we were truly celebrating, and helped me develop a close relationship between my Savior and me during the Christmas season."

– Rachel

Finding the
Treasure in Christmas

Advent Traditions for Families with Kids of All Ages

By John S. Lewis

Finding the Treasure in Christmas:
Advent Traditions for Families with Kids of all Ages
Third Edition Trade Book 2022

ISBN: 978-0-9998362-6-2

Also available by John S. Lewis:
Experiencing the Passion and Purpose of the Cross
The Kingdom Story and The Kingdom Story: Study Version

Editorial:	Inspira Literary Solutions, Gig Harbor, Washington; Jennifer Tabert, Seattle, Washington
Book Design:	Cody Lail, Tacoma, Washington; Holly Knoll, Left Corner Design

Acknowledgments

Many thanks to the legion of advice givers, editors, and proofreaders over the years who have made each version of this book better than the last: Arlyn Lawrence and Kerry Wade at Inspira Literary Solutions, Marty Kelly, Emily Bosh, Steve Hauge, Corinne Pingel, Sharon Cantrill, Jennifer Tabert, Maril Walle, and Branden Hubbell. Thanks to Cody Lail and Holly Knoll who helped in the graphic design and in merging the original two volumes into one.

Many thanks to my own three kids for their enthusiasm (and patience!) for my Advent experiments. A big and heartfelt thanks to my wife Carissa for her contagious holiday passion, editing help, and divinely energized patience through each revision. Thanks lastly to the many family members, neighbors, and friends who joined us to celebrate and make memories along the way.

Dedication

This guide for making family Advent traditions is dedicated to my three children and to the One whom we have celebrated and waited for every Christmas: Jesus Christ.

Table of Contents

WEEK 1: JESUS IS THE TREE OF LIFE & THE LIGHT OF THE WORLD

WEEK 2: JESUS WAS BORN AS ONE OF US

WEEK 3: WE GIVE BECAUSE GOD GAVE FIRST

WEEK 4: THE STAR & ANGELS POINT TO JESUS

Finding the
Treasure in Christmas

Advent Traditions for Families with Kids of All Ages

By John S. Lewis

Advent Traditions

This book was designed to help your family make Christmas traditions for many years and Advent seasons to come! To help make this book the family treasure it is designed to be, pages in the back have been added for photos, highlights, and memories from each Christmas season.

Cover from the first Lewis Advent Book in 2003

Why Create Advent Traditions?

THE FOCUS OF CHRISTMAS

Many of my warmest childhood Christmas memories are connected to the traditions of Christmas: putting up our tree, hanging ornaments, putting up lights, hanging the star, opening my stocking, and unwrapping my gifts. However, I have no memories of being told how all these could help me better understand or celebrate the real meaning of Christmas.

At church, we sang about the Bethlehem story, but we never connected the symbols I loved— Santa and Christmas trees, the presents and stockings, candy canes and Christmas lights— with the coming of God into the world as one of us. This created an unfortunate disconnect for me. All this was also true for my wife, Carissa.

We wanted our children to see the beauty of Jesus' birth story throughout the season. We learned to eliminate the disconnect between so many of the traditional practices of the Christmas season and the meaning of the Christmas story.

As we set out to reconnect them, we discovered that many of the season's most beloved symbols and practices originally had strong Christian roots that could be reclaimed, or easily infused, with the original meaning of the Christmas story.

Today, amidst our family schedules, various demands, and nagging interruptions, many of us are easily distracted from the treasures of life. This is perhaps never truer than during Christmas, as the meaning of the holiday has become more and more hidden. We believe it is both valuable and important that we commit to the work of unburying the riches in Christmas and its symbols.

THE PURPOSE OF ADVENT

Advent is the four-week season before Christmas, traditionally recognized as an extended time of reflection on "the Coming" of Jesus into our world. But sometimes, the holiday hustle can make us feel just like those who missed the First Coming of baby Jesus. What should be so central seems the most easily overlooked.

For followers of Jesus, our intentional remembering is perhaps the most important part of getting ready for Christmas.

Our first model for remembering Christ's birth is Mary, Jesus' mother. On the night he was born, she is said to have "treasured all these things in her heart." Undoubtedly, she held dear the memories all mothers do, but that cannot be all. She treasured the truth about this unique baby: the miraculous visit from an angel, the divine conception, the baby leaping in her cousin Elizabeth's womb, angels heralding Heaven's hymns to the shepherds in the night, and Magi dumbstruck by a star they could not help but follow.

Mary showed deep wisdom by choosing to ponder and treasure these memories in her heart.

In the spirit of Mary, Advent invites us to set aside moments to ponder and treasure this mystery in our own homes and hearts. And while it may have come naturally to Mary, for most of us living in today's world a more sustained effort is required. Beginning and protecting family traditions can lead to a fulfillment of what our families long for most at Christmas: connection with God and each other and an understanding of the true gift of the season.

WHY TRADITIONS MATTER

The church's historic observance of Advent was instituted for the same reason God wanted Israel to celebrate feasts and holidays: so that God's followers could take time to remember him and reconnect to their identity as his people. Unlike many of us living in North America, a melting pot of cultures, the Jews were committed to remaining a holy people set aside from the nations around them. If there had been no Sabbath with its mandated rest, no Passover feast with its rich symbols and no holidays with community storytelling of their heritage, the Jews would have quickly assimilated into the surrounding culture. They would have dissolved as God's people and become lost to history.

In revisiting and retelling the central stories of their faith, Jewish parents passed down to the next generation the foundations upon which to build their lives in a foreign land. In their annual feast of Passover, Jewish parents and children remembered God's deliverance with the same foods, prayers, and rites as in years before. They did so not just for nostalgia's sake but in the belief that Yahweh, their Redeemer, was again present in their current suffering.

God's gift of sabbath and festival traditions was part of the glue that held the Jewish people together during exile and persecution. Today, those parents who want their children's love for God to endure for a lifetime in today's world, family faith traditions remain a valuable tool.

Advent traditions help shape our children's hearts, enrich our family's faith, and prepare us to be Christ's light in a world that has largely forgotten the Jesus story. Because God Emmanuel came to be with us that first Christmas, we can know he is still very much with us this Christmas.

In the meantime, we hold on to the hope that he is coming again on that final Christmas day.

MAKE A PLAN

Christmas is a full and active time, so we have sought to find a flexible way of celebrating without feeling overwhelmed or disjointed. Yet as open-handed and fun as we tried to make our Advent traditions, none of our efforts were without prioritizing, planning, and protecting. There were times we had to say no to genuinely good holiday expectations and possibilities. Otherwise, with the Advent activities added, our family's "Christmas ship" would have sunk in overload.

And so, each year, we stumbled forward in the messiness and the wonder of the season. Our Christmas traditions helped lead our family into an annual rediscovery of the treasure of Christmas, and perhaps to better live in that treasure all year long. Remembering the Christ of Christmas each year is serious business.

How to Use This Book

WHAT

The celebration of Advent helps develop traditions and memories to return your family to the heart of the Christmas story. This book gives you a breadth of activities to help your family build traditions in a flexible and creative way. It is not a workbook to complete.

We highly recommend you order a copy of **The New Guideposts' Christmas Treasury.** Our family loved these stories; the one chosen for each day of this book in some way relates to the theme (see Appendix). Read year after year, these stories added a sparkle to our home's Advent traditions

HOW OFTEN

While this book can be used as a one-time experience, it was designed to help families build traditions and faith-forming memories year after year. Using a book only one year can't make that happen. Forming meaningful traditions requires repetition.

WHO

While this Advent book can be used and modified for Sunday school classes, couples, small groups, larger church gatherings, and even personal devotions, its most natural use is in the home. This book is targeted towards adults and families with kids from age two to eighteen.

WHEN

Begin this book on the first Sunday of Advent and continue through Christmas Eve. Sundays are typically the easist day to anchor Advent in the home and you'll want to plan on thirty to forty minutes for activities, if you can (up to an hour if your kids are old enough). The weekday readings and activities are intended to last about fifteen minutes.

Symbols and Themes for Each Week

WEEK ONE: TREES & LIGHTS

This week highlights the larger story of our faith, from creation to the Second Coming of Christ.

WEEK TWO: ORNAMENTS & NATIVITY

This week emphasizes Jesus as Emmanuel, "God with us." Jesus was, and still is, present in the relationships and realities all humans share.

WEEK THREE: GIFTS & STOCKINGS

This week reminds us that our tradition of giving presents at Christmas comes from the spirit of the Magi's gifts: we give to each other because God first gave us Jesus.

WEEK FOUR: STAR & ANGELS

As the stars and angels guided the characters of the Christmas story, so Jesus still goes ahead of us and guides us through the darkness of our life journey.

FOCUS

Each day will have a title and focus related to the Christmas symbols and theme of the week. This focus includes something important for our lives all year long.

READ

One or two Bible passages are given for reading. Included are both the classic Christmas stories and also other biblical passages. To get our post-preschool children more involved, we had our kids look up and read the passages themselves; sometimes they even acted out the story.

REFLECT

This is a short reflection relating to the theme of the day, written with slightly older children and adults in mind. Parents can skip or paraphrase this section for younger children.

SHARE

Activities or discussion questions related to the day's theme are offered for Monday to Saturday. The questions after "Ask" are meant to be read aloud directly to your kids.

Because this book was designed to be used in a family over many years, the three sharing questions are appropriate for, and usually broken into, three age brackets:

- Young children (roughly ages 2-4)
- Older children (roughly ages 5-12)
- Teenagers (roughly ages 13-18)

SING

This is a verse from a classic Christmas carol. There is often a connection of the carol's words to the scripture or focus of the day.

PRAY

There will be a short prayer provided for you to use directly—feel free to alter it, or offer your own.

SUNDAYS

Because families might more easily make Sunday their special Advent celebration day, you will find some extra activities on this day.

On Sunday you will be invited to decorate your home with the common Christmas symbols that will be highlighted and reflected upon during the week.

LIGHTING THE ADVENT CANDLE

Here you will find a brief explanation of the week's Advent candle. Procure an Advent wreath and candles ahead of time.

OTHER OPTIONS

These are extra options for Sunday or other week days, for those who want to experiment or change up the routine.

WATCH

Here you will find one or more classic Christmas shows or movies to watch on Sunday or any day of the week. Included is a brief explanation of how the movie relates to the week's theme.

CONNECT TO OTHERS

This will discuss a way to deepen your family's celebration of Advent and present an idea of how to extend God's gift and the spirit of Advent to your neighborhood and community. This can be accomplished any time during the week.

Pray

Father God, may the simplicity of Christ's birth warm our hearts again this Christmas season. Help us to celebrate as if we were having a birthday party, and so much more, because we are. Let the mysteries of your Son's coming awaken deep awe in us. May our Advent experience help bind our lives with faith and hope in you. Let the Christmas message hold us in wonder all year long.

Amen.

WEEK ONE

JESUS IS THE TREE OF LIFE
THE LIGHT OF THE WORLD

For the Day You Put Up the Tree

CHRISTMAS TRADITION

Go to a tree farm, or tree lot, or take out your family Christmas tree and put it up.

Our family's tradition was to bundle up and climb into a neighbor's pickup truck and head out the Saturday after Thanksgiving to go cut down our tree at a local tree farm. If your family goes to a tree lot or just uses an artificial tree, you may enjoy this bonus page.

READ

Gather and read **Philippians 2: 5-7**

REFLECT

The heart and start of Christmas is God's costly decision to send His Son to Earth to be among us.

Christmas trees are cut down and taken from their biological home in nature. In a sense they "give up their life" so that we can enjoy a beautifully decorated Christmas tree in our home. It is only because of our tree's "death" that we can easily see its beauty and fragrance in the familiarity of where we live.

Similarly, it wasn't natural for him to become a human and dwell among us. Jesus decided to leave what was familiar in heaven to be with us. In doing so Jesus made it easier for us to see and relate to God. And like the tree whose days are numbered once it is cut, so Jesus' days were few and numbered before his life was taken.

So again this holiday season, when we look at our Christmas tree, let's be reminded that Jesus left his home and gave his life so that we could be in relationship together.

I GIVE MY LIFE

A Poem by Rachel Lewis

I am tall and proud
I am a ladder that can't be climbed
I reach up to the Heavens
I am beautiful.

I dance in the wind
I sing in the rain
I smile in the sun
I sigh in the snow.

They come together
They glance, their furrowed brows,
Sunny smiles, ringing laughs
Fingers of rain touch me.

Standing like a tower
Seeing sharp clawed hands
Pleading to live
Gasping for breath.

Leaving everything,
My comforting home below
Fresh breath around me
My own little Heaven.

Desperately dying
Snapping limbs
Pain shooting up my now withering body
Yet the laughter inside keeps me living.

Twisted, turning, down, down
Lifted, carried, balanced
Rest at last covers me like a soft blanket
A drink like a cool mountain spring.

Small tender hands upon me
And mellow sleepy lights
Oohs and ahs like a soft sweet song
Carrying precious gifts upon me.

Loved at last
Like none but me
My death worth it
I would do it all again.

SING

O Christmas Tree

O Christmas tree, o Christmas tree
How lovely are thy branches
O Christmas tree, o Christmas tree
How lovely are thy branches

Your boughs so green in summertime
Stay bravely green in wintertime
O Christmas tree, o Christmas tree
How lovely are thy branches

PRAY

Jesus, we praise you for leaving your natural place in Heaven and coming at such a great cost to dwell on earth in a human body. Thank you for making it possible for us to see and know God in such a special way. You knew we needed you to come; thank you for still coming through your Spirit into the familiar places where we live, work, learn and love. Amen.

1. Watch *How the Grinch Stole Christmas*, 1966. (Note the theme of the light and life of Christmas not being found in material things, but in the heart.)

2. Take a nighttime walk around your neighborhood. Enjoy the Christmas lights, stop by a house, or sing a carol. If they are old enough, let the kids hold flashlights as a sign that you are God's light. Pray for your neighbors as you walk.

3. Hang up inside/outside lights. When it becomes dark, shut off all the house lights. Sit in darkness for a moment, and then plug in your lights. Imagine the lights are like Jesus bringing light into the world when he was born.

4. Read a suggested story from the *New Guideposts Christmas Treasury*, found in Appendix II.

Jesus Is the Tree of Life, the Light of the World

FOCUS

Our green Christmas tree reminds us that Jesus brings life to our world and to our home. As we look at our Christmas lights, we are also reminded of two things: first, that Jesus is the Light of the World, and second, that he in turn calls us to be lights to the world.

TRADITIONS AND ACTIVITIES

1. Make or buy your Advent wreath and find a central place for it in your home.

2. Set up your tree. You might pick out a fresh tree from a tree farm or tree lot or bring out your artificial tree from storage; no matter the process, we can still be reminded of Jesus' story. If you go out to buy or cut a fresh tree see the previous page.

3. Light the first Advent candle, the "Prophecy Candle." Read Isaiah 9:2 and 11:1 as you do. These verses are prophecies about the future spoken hundreds of years before Jesus was born. Notice how Isaiah 9:2 mentions people walking in darkness will see a great light. Isaiah 11:1 metaphorically promises that a shoot of new green life will come up from God's people who appeared to be just a dead stump. As we light the first advent candle, we are reminded that God brought, and still brings, both his light and life to the world.

REFLECT

Every year, our family's first Advent tradition is to cut down our tree, put it up in our house, and decorate it with lights. But where did this familiar tradition come from? Legend has it that centuries ago, on a Christmas Eve night, the theologian Martin Luther looked up at the forest, seeing the trees with the moon and stars behind them. Inspired by this beautiful scene, he introduced the tradition of the Christmas tree and candles. The green pine tree, already a recognized symbol of life in ancient Druid festivals, became a symbol for Christ's abundant and everlasting life. The candles symbolized Jesus, the Light of the world.

Though the rich greenness of a Christmas tree stands in bold contrast to the stark landscape of Jesus' homeland in Israel, the stars over ancient Bethlehem would have shone brightly in the countryside darkness.

The two Isaiah prophecies were fulfilled in Jesus' coming. In his teaching and preaching Jesus brought his light of truth to minds and hearts darkened by sin. In his miracles he brought life to the sick, the stuck and the aimless. The Apostle John summarized how Jesus did that in John 1:4, "In him was life, and the life was the light of us all."

Yes, Jesus was a gift of light and life. What a gift he was and is! The line from "How the Grinch Stole Christmas" perfectly sums up our wish for Advent: "Welcome Christmas, bring your light."

SING

Hark, the Herald Angels Sing (Verse 3)

Hail the Heaven-born Prince of Peace!
Hail the Son of Righteousness!
Light and life to all He brings,
Risen with healing in His wings.

Mild He lays His glory by,
Born that man no more may die,
Born to raise the sons of earth,
Born to give them second birth.
Hark! The herald angels sing,
"Glory to the newborn King!"

PRAY

Lord, your light is greater than our darkness and shows us the way. Your life is greater than what our world and its ways could ever offer us. Thank you, God, for being full of life and light, and thank you for Jesus, who shared both of these gifts with us. May our lights and tree remind us of this daily. Help us to receive your light and life and then share them with others. Amen.

Jesus Is the Light and Life of Creation

FOCUS

At the beginning of the Bible story, God creates light and living things to fill the Earth. We are to remember that God still gives light and life to us today!

READ

Open to **Genesis 1:1–5, 11 and 2:4–9, 15–17** (verses most related to light and life). A fun idea might be to start reading this scripture in the dark with a flashlight, then turn on the lights when you get to the part where God creates light.

REFLECT

This week's symbols of light and trees show up repeatedly in the Bible, from Genesis to Revelation. This week we will follow these themes throughout the grand sweep of the entire Bible story. Let's start at the beginning.

Just as each day begins at midnight in darkness, the creation story in Genesis also starts in chaos and darkness. Then, God speaks light into existence (1:3). This light creates the possibility of life for plants, animals, and us.

Trees were also part of God's rich creation. Eden was tucked in the middle of a desert where water was scarce and fruitful trees were signs of extravagant life. God's first command was for the woman and the man to eat their fill as often as they liked from these fruit-bearing trees.

Just as we place our Christmas trees in the center of our homes, God placed the Tree of Life and the Tree of the Knowledge of Good and Evil in the center of the garden, in the middle of Adam and Eve's daily living. In declaring the second tree off-limits, God made the boundaries to his love and generosity clear. Only in trusting and obeying God would Adam and Eve truly enjoy their Creator's gift of true life. And what a life God had in store for them in Eden's abundance.

And who was there with God the Father, co-creating life and light, trees and abundant vegetation? God's son, Jesus Christ. When Jesus eventually came to Earth in human form, it was to continue the work both he and the Father began long before any of us were created. No wonder we call Jesus the Light of the World and Giver of Life.

For those who put their trust in God, Jesus is still bringing abundant life out of chaos and light out of darkness. Through this grace, we are grafted into God's strong tree of life. Without Jesus, we are like a balloon without air, a light bulb without a socket, a puppet without a hand. "In him we live and move and have our being" (Acts 17:28).

SHARE

Read and then discuss the question or questions that are best suited for the ages of your children.

1. Have everyone draw a favorite plant and/or animal that God created in the beginning and that he still creates.

2. Unplug the tree's lights and turn off the room lights. Ask: *What would the world be like without the sun or any other kind of light? What would happen to the plants? Our food? Our life?* Remember together: the only way we, too, can truly live is in the light of God's "Son."

3. God's first and generous command is literally to "Eat, eat of every tree of the garden." Ask: *What do you imagine his tone of voice and the expression on his face were when God said this?* Have everyone share a specific example of how you experienced God's generosity and life this last year.

SING

O Christmas Tree

O Christmas tree, o Christmas tree
How lovely are thy branches
O Christmas tree, o Christmas tree
How lovely are thy branches

Your boughs so green in summertime
Stay bravely green in wintertime
O Christmas tree, o Christmas tree
How lovely are thy branches

PRAY

Thank you, God, for making each of us, and breathing the breath of life in this beautiful world and in beautiful me! Everything would be so different without the abundant life and light you give to us. We are so glad you are good and take care of everything you made. Help us to keep you as central in our lives as our Christmas tree is in our home this season. Amen.

Light and Life Became Dim Through Sin

FOCUS

When Adam and Eve disobeyed God, they were surrounded by darkness and felt lost and afraid. When we disobey God, we can feel the same way, and that we, too, are trapped in the dark. This is why God would later send Jesus to bring us light and make us alive again.

READ

Turn off all the lights and use a candle or a flashlight to read **Genesis 3:1-13, 22-24**.

REFLECT

After the world was created, God made Adam and Eve to live in the Garden of Eden. However, it did not take long for God's paradise to experience disaster. The serpent's question about God's command and stinginess clouded Eve's ability to see clearly and trust God's words. She believed the lies and ate the fruit, hoping for true life in each forbidden bite. Unfortunately, Eve found herself in darkness and death, hiding from her husband in shame.

Where was Adam all this time? Right beside his wife. He, too, was fooled by the serpent's false promises. He joined Eve in disobeying God's loving and serious commandment, "Don't eat from the Tree of the Knowledge of Good and Evil." The Lord kept true to his word and sent the man and woman out of the privileged place of Eden's full pleasure.

The Lord's mercy made sure that death did not have the last word. Despite their rebellion, God still approached Adam and Eve right after their sin in the cool of the day. The consequences of their sin were serious but not fatal; they would be allowed to live and still enjoy many of Earth's blessings, though now under the curse of broken relationships.

Adam and Eve traded in extravagance for existence as the central experience of life, and the world has never recovered. We, too, live under sin's consequences. We might appear to ourselves or others like the Christmas trees in our living rooms, to be fully alive, but in reality, we are already drying up and doomed to death.

But thankfully, because of God's great love for us, we are not left in death and darkness! It is only by God's mercy that our sin does not cut us off completely from the spring of his living water. God's light makes a blazing comeback throughout the rest of the story—and the rest of human history. That is what Christmas is all about.

SHARE

Read and then discuss the question or questions that are best suited for the ages of your child(ren).

1. Have everyone hang up a plain red ornament on the tree, which is traditionally a symbol of sin. Looking at these red ornaments in the weeks ahead will remind us of Adam and Eve's disobedience, our own sin, and why Jesus needed to bring us life and light.

2. Turn out all the house and Christmas lights. Sit for a moment in the dark. Ask: *why are people afraid of the dark? What are some ways people experience darkness in their lives?*
Then turn on the lights and be thankful Jesus does not leave us in our sin and darkness!

3. Recall from our story together what Adam and Eve did, or did not do, that harmed their relationships with God and each other. Ask: *What is one personal example from the last year where your sin had a negative effect on your relationship with either someone close to you or with God?*

4. Review together what Adam and Eve did after they ate the forbidden fruit: they hid, blamed others, and felt shame. Ask: *What is an example from your current relationships or in our culture where you see the same consequences happening: hiding, blame, shame?*

SING

O Holy Night

O Holy Night!
The stars are brightly shining
It is the night of the dear Savior's birth!
Long lay the world in sin and error pining
Till He appear'd and the soul felt its worth.
A thrill of hope, the weary world rejoices
For yonder breaks
a new and glorious morn!

PRAY

Lord, from the very beginning of time, Adam and Eve's story has been our story too. We are tempted to think we can see without your light, that we can be joyful and happy with something besides you. Sometimes, when we recognize our sin, we feel ashamed and far from you and each other. The world has needed a Savior since Adam and Eve. Come, Lord Jesus, and change our death into life and bring your light to our darkness. Amen.

The Light and Life Were God's Special Promise

FOCUS

After Adam and Eve sinned, God made a plan to save them—and everyone else. God's plan started with Abraham and included men like Moses and David and women like Ruth and Esther. God's tribe Israel and its leaders did not always love God or obey his commands. Still, God gave his people a promise to make all things well in the future by sending us his Son as a baby.

READ

Read the first half of both **Isaiah 7:14 and 49:6**. Then read **Jeremiah 33:15-16**, a less-well-known prophecy from the time of Israel's captivity in Babylon. All of them refer to either the image of light or the tree in predicting the coming of the Messiah, Jesus Christ.

REFLECT

When Cain, the son of Adam and Eve, killed his brother, the fruit of sin was passed on from one generation to the next. By Noah's lifetime, life on Earth had soured so badly that God sent a flood to restart the world. When Noah's descendants once again rebelled and sought to build a tower to heaven on their own (i.e., the Tower of Babel), God didn't give up. A plan was brewing.

In his promise to Abraham, God planted a seed of hope by setting aside a small clan of people with a special mission. These people, Abraham's descendants, were to become a nation that would shine his shining light to the whole world.

But God's people never responded well to his overtures of love and purpose. They even worshipped a golden calf on Mt. Sinai after their "wedding day." After centuries of disobedience and idolatry, the Lord brought the powerful nations of Assyria and Babylon to humble and overcome them. What seemed to them as rightful punishment for their sins was much more: Israel's failures only led them to later see God's extraordinary faithfulness to call them back home.

When God's "vine" Israel found herself as exiled and captives in Babylon, she heard a whisper of hope, a promise of a coming king. A righteous "branch" would rise from the stump of the nation left by God's judgment. Those living in the darkness of doubt and despair were promised a magnificent Messiah.

No king in Israel's history, not even David in all his glory, came close to fulfilling the Old Testament prophecy found in Jeremiah 33:15-16. Only centuries later would this promised branch come from David's line and be born in Bethlehem. His arrival is the next chapter of God's beautiful salvation story.

SHARE

Read and then discuss the question or questions that are best suited for the age of your child(ren).

1. Have each person in your family hang on your tree a plain red ornament. Each one represents the people of Israel's sins, some of which were discussed in the Reflect section. Optional: recount together one example of sin in the Old Testament for each red ornament. As you do so, remember that their sin is also our sin. We all need Jesus to come and bring us light and life.

2. Play a short game of charades. On separate slips of paper, write down a few Old Testament stories that everyone knows where a single person or Israel as a group committed a sin (e.g., Cain murdering Abel, people building the Tower of Babel, Aaron and the Israelites making the Golden Calf, Esau stealing his brother's blessing).

SING

O Come, O Come, Immanuel

O come, O come, Immanuel,
and ransom captive Israel
that mourns in lonely exile here
until the Son of God appear.

Rejoice! Rejoice! Immanuel
shall come to you, O Israel.

PRAY

Thank you, God, for never leaving your people Israel, no matter how many times they failed to obey you. Your promises were so precious to them and still are to us today. Thank you for keeping them by sending Jesus, the Light of the World, and for loving us forever. Amen.

Light and Life Came through Jesus

FOCUS

Jesus came into the world as a baby, fully human just like us. He came as a fragile, helpless infant who had the most important work to do that had ever been done or ever will be done. His important job would be to save us from darkness, to make us clean from sin, and to live inside us.

READ

Open the Bible to **Luke 2:25-33**.

REFLECT

December's days are the darkest of the year in the northern hemisphere. We eagerly anticipate the coming tide of spring when the weight of darkness will once more be lifted. In a similar way, the cycle of death and spiritual darkness was broken by the coming of the Christ child. Jesus ushered in a new season of light for us all.

Even as a baby, Jesus' light and glory shone on those who saw him. In our scripture, something special happened when Joseph and Mary brought their newborn to the temple for circumcision. The old and holy man Simeon had waited long to see the Messiah before he died. After one glimpse of Jesus, the Spirit helped him see what child this was: this was the promised One who would grow up to be the light that would reveal God's salvation. He would make God's new life available to even the farthest nations.

Simeon did not live to see it, but he could die in peace and confidence. Thirty years later, Jesus indeed brought life to those wearied by despair and, a few times, to those already dead and buried. His light brought sight to the physically blind. It brought understanding to those who labored under the heavy lie that they must do the right thing in order to be loved by God.

Then, in the unnatural afternoon darkness of Good Friday, Jesus died on Calvary's hill. On that cross, the Lamb of God as our Savior bore in his body all the sins of the past, present, and future. Bearing the consequence of our sin temporarily extinguished his life and light. Three days later, on that first Easter Sunday, Jesus rose in the fullness of life. And after he ascended to heaven, the Father sent the Spirit of Jesus to bring life and light to all who follow him.

The early church grew upon this cornerstone, witnessing firsthand the light of Christ's resurrection. The Jews were the first to say yes to God's future plans, but soon people from surrounding nations joined in, too. Christ's victory opened salvation's door wide forever. Now all people from every nation are welcomed into this new chapter of God's light in the world.

No wonder we call him Jesus, which means in Greek, "God saves!"

SHARE

Read and then discuss the question or questions that are best suited for the age of your child(ren).

1. Sit quietly for a few minutes as a family in a dark room. Then have an adult or an older child come in from another room with a lit candle. Thank Jesus together for being the Light who came into our dark world.

2. Sit quietly together looking at the tree and its lights, which represent Jesus. Then together share several ways Jesus brought life and light to the world when he first came to Earth.

3. Jesus still brings light and life to his people like he did when he first came. Ask: *What is one way Jesus brought his light and life into our family this last year? (Parents can share before children.)*

SING

What Child is This?

What Child is this who, laid to rest
On Mary's lap, is sleeping?
Whom angels greet with anthems sweet
While shepherds watch are keeping?
This, this is Christ the King,
Whom shepherds guard and angels sing,
Haste, haste, to bring Him laud,
The Babe, the Son of Mary!

PRAY

Thank you, Father God, for sending Jesus to give us life and to be the Light of the World. It is amazing that your Son was fully human and began his time on Earth as a baby, just like us. Thank you, God, also for using the darkness of Jesus' death as a door to bring us life. And thank you, Jesus, that you still bring light to us, even in darkness, in both simple and amazing ways! Amen.

Light and Life Are Shared by All God's People

FOCUS

In the Christmas story, it was the shepherds' important job to show others that Jesus was the Light and Life of the World. They proclaimed the good news to their friends in the hope that the entire world would know about God's Son. We have the same important job as the shepherds and the early church: we are to share his light and life to the world!

READ

Read **Luke 2:13-18; Matthew 5:13-15**. Plug in a string of lights and put them under your couch/chair before the Matthew 5:13-15 reading, and then pull them out as you read it for fun/impact.

REFLECT

Who are we? Why are we here? To these age-old questions, Jesus gives us his enduring response: "We are here to be the salt of the earth. We are the Light of the world." Those who follow Jesus do indeed have a high calling.

But what does it mean to be salt and light? People in the ancient world primarily used salt like modern people often use a refrigerator. Without salt, food rotted. With salt, their food was preserved, flavorful and life-giving. When we are filled with God's presence and power, our involvement in the rotting places of this world brings the life of Christ. Evil will still often seem stronger than good, but how much worse would the world be without God's salt?

Secondly, we are to be the Light of the world. The shepherds almost immediately told everyone about the light that shone on Bethlehem's baby, in a way that amazed those who heard them. In the same way, followers of Jesus are to proclaim to others what we ourselves have seen, heard, and touched (1 John 1:1-4). As the classic American Sunday school song goes, "This little light of mine, I'm going to let it shine!"

But people will not hear our words well unless they first see our love. God promises that when we love one another, people will witness Christ in us. Other people will not easily see or believe God without the church living out a compelling example in this world. Notice the difference between Christ's words and the song: not "I" but "we" are the light of the world. Hear the song redone: *"This little light of ours, we're going to let it shine!"* His light shines through us to reveal Jesus to the world when we love each other and our neighbor. Because Christ dwells in us, we are his salt and light in the world. What an honorable mission we have inherited!

SHARE

Read and then discuss the question or questions that are best suited for the age of your child(ren).

1. Be a light to one of your neighbors by visiting and wishing them a Merry Christmas.

2. After dark, have one person turn off all the inside and outside lights. Go outside together and stand in front of the window where your tree and inside lights are kept. Have one person go back in the house and turn on the indoor Christmas lights. As these lights draw you to look inside the house, God's people are to be a light as well. People who see us should soon want to look at Christ, the Light of the World.

3. Do, or plan to do, Sunday's **Connect to Others** option or discuss with your kids one practical and simple way either they alone or together as a family, can be God's light to someone this Christmas season. Make a plan and follow through, but also be open to a spontaneous opportunity.

SING

Go Tell It On The Mountain

Go tell it on the mountain
Over the hills and everywhere
Go tell it on the mountain
Our Jesus Christ is born!

When I was a seeker
I sought both night and day
I asked the Lord to help me
And he showed me the way.

PRAY

Father God, thank you for having Jesus, the Life and Light of the world, now live inside the church through your Spirit. Lord, when we are "plugged in" to you, it's your plan that we also be your light in the world. Thank you for this important job. Teach us this Christmas season and all year long how we can help other people see you in us! Amen.

Light and Life Will Be Perfect in Heaven

FOCUS

One day, Jesus will come back again, not as a baby or a normal human being, but as an amazing King, full of life and light! When Jesus does come back, Heaven will finally come to Earth.

READ

Open to **Isaiah 9:5-6** and **Revelation 22:1-5**.

REFLECT

When the angels' song rang out, the shepherds caught a glimpse of eternity, an image and a sound from the fringes of Heaven. A year earlier, Mary received a similar glimpse of eternity when the angel told her of Jesus' future reign of greatness (Luke 1:32-33).

Today, we need a longer look at Jesus' Second Coming; again, the coming of Jesus in the past as a baby is a prelude to his crucial Second Coming and establishing his kingdom fully on earth.

The truth is, many of us would rather not think about the fact that our days are as numbered as pre-cut Christmas trees. We would often rather fall into only the past focus of Christmas, which has come to dominate the Advent season in many churches today. Yet the rise of the world's chaos ought to welcome Advent's focus on the Second Coming, the "future Christmas."

The angel's message to Mary (Luke 1:32-33) and the book of Revelation shed light on this vision of God's future: the risen Jesus will reign forever! The Christ who came to die in weakness will return as both roaring Lion and risen Lamb. Jesus' name will be great and his kingdom will never end. The river of life flowing from his throne will water trees that bear fruit in great abundance. Leaves from these trees will bring life and healing to every wound. The sun will be no more as it is no longer needed; Jesus will be the light of all. The God who was previously unapproachable will be accessible in the New Jerusalem garden (1 Timothy 6:16, Revelation 21:1-2).

The long-ago spoken words of the angel to the shepherds will fully come true: "Peace on Earth among those whom God favors."

Bought with the precious life of the Lamb, we will one day join Jesus, walking through the open door to this eternal paradise. If our advent hope of the future is true, life on Earth is just a dress rehearsal.

So as we celebrate the First Coming of Christ at Christmas, we also wait. We wait and long for his Second Coming and future restoration of all things. This future is what Christmas is all about.

SHARE

Read and then discuss the question or questions that are best suited for the age of your child(ren).

1. Discuss and then draw one thing that your family thinks will be part of Heaven when it comes down to make the Earth new (e.g., abundant sunshine, plentiful food).

2. Draw together one or two parts from the Revelation 22:1–5 description of Heaven coming to Earth. Then remember that the same God who promised that Jesus would come the first time also promised that Jesus would surely come again to bring Heaven on Earth.

3. Take some time together to be quiet before the tree and lights, in a posture of listening and waiting for the return of Jesus. In silence, reflect on how the same God who promised Jesus would come the first time also promised that his Son would surely come again.

SING

Joy to the World (Verse 2)

Joy to the World, the Savior reigns!
Let men their songs employ;
While fields and floods, rocks, hills and plains
Repeat the sounding joy. (x3)

PRAY

Thank you, God, for promising to come back someday to Earth to make everything new and beautiful. Until that day arrives, help us see the ways that Heaven is already here in your kingdom. Help us get ourselves and the world ready for your Second Coming. Amen.

JESUS CAME AS ONE OF US

1. Watch *Frosty the Snowman,*
   1969. (Notice the theme of
   snow coming to life and then
   melting to symbolize Christ's
   incarnation, death, and
   resurrection.)

2. Use the globe or a world map
   to pray for people of a different
   culture and with different needs
   than yours.

3. Read a suggested story from
   *The New Guideposts Christmas
   Treasury,* found in Appendix II.

Jesus Was Born as One of Us

FOCUS

God came as a baby so he could live the full human
experience and grow up from child to adult, just as we do.
Our Nativity set and ornaments remind us that Jesus had a
birth story, a significant birthplace, and a childhood with a
special family. Jesus was, in so many ways, just like us!

TRADITIONS AND ACTIVITIES

1. Put up some or all of your ornaments.

2. If you have a Nativity set, set it up today.

3. Light the second Advent candle, called the
   "Bethlehem Candle." In this little, ordinary town,
   we will find all the earthly details of Jesus and his
   coming. Read John 1:14 after you light the candle,
   about Jesus, the Word, becoming flesh.

REFLECT

Our tree holds family ornaments we ourselves have
bought or made, some are gifts from others. Some are
plain or ornamental, some are in honor of one of our
children, some were bought in places we have visited and
hold memories we don't want to forget.

Each year as the kids grew up we added new ornaments,
filling our tree with memories.

When we decorate the tree, then, we remember the
people, places, and particulars of our family's story.

That's why our ornaments made our family's Christmas tree unique.

Ornaments can also remind us that Jesus' birth story is full of unique and significant details. Jesus was born in the town of Bethlehem, in the small backwater country of Israel. He arrived on a particular day and year sometime around 4 BC. In the Nativity, we see baby Jesus in swaddling clothes, laying in the manger, and the shepherds from a nearby field who all ran to see him first. These elements all point us to the truth that Christmas is rooted in a story; Jesus' birth story, like all good stories, is full of details.

When we put up our ornaments and Nativity set, we once again remember John's famous words: "the Word once became flesh and dwelt among us." In a way, Jesus was God's "ornament" for us all to see. The Lord came to Earth as a child—an adopted child even—so people could see God in all the particulars of Jesus' everyday life. His glory became inseparable with the ordinary routines of eating and cleaning, listening and learning, working and playing.

Here is the good news: Jesus came embedded in a time and a place. He, the sinless King of Glory, experienced all the everyday details of life so that we could have a new perspective on every detail and aspect of our lives today. The places and people of every culture, the ordinary and sometimes dreary circumstances of life—all of these matter to God.

We, members of Christ's body, are also God's ornaments.

SING

O Come All Ye Faithful (Verse 3)

Yea, Lord, we greet Thee,
Born this happy morning;
Jesus, to Thee be glory given!
Word of the Father,
Now in flesh appearing!

(Chorus) O come, let us adore Him, (x3)
Christ the Lord.

PRAY

Creator God, in dogs and dolphins, strawberries and sunshine, rivers and rabbits, you have always made it clear that you are full of life. Thank you, Jesus, for coming to us fully human and fully divine, full of light and life. For all the life and light you have shown us through people, relationships, and circumstances, we thank you. Remind us through our ornaments and our Nativity set that we, like you, were born to a special family, place, and time. Amen.

41

Jesus Came as a Baby

FOCUS

People love babies and are filled with joy when they are around them. God wants us, and the whole world, to be joyful about Jesus coming into the world as a baby, as one of us!

READ

Open the Bible to **Luke 2:4-7, 19.**

REFLECT

When God sent his Son to Earth, he did not come as a mysterious spirit, an impersonal force, or a dramatic firework show in the sky. Jesus emptied himself of his divine privileges and slipped into the world in the likeness of human being. Yes, the Son of God arrived here not as a majestic warrior but as the angel promised to favored Mary: a gentle baby, her first born son.

In the Hebrew way of thinking, all this was impossible; even to suggest something like it would have been a scandal. Before Jesus, God's name could not even be mentioned, his presence could not be endured, and his face could not be seen without certain death. Only once a year could the high priest walk backwards into the Holy of Holies to encounter God. The thought of God coming as a lowly human, someone they could talk to and touch and interact with on a daily basis, was too radical to ever enter their imaginations.

Mary, Jesus' mother, was of course one of the first to see Jesus, the baby. What a sight he must have been to her as she laid the Son of God in that Bethlehem manger. No wonder she long pondered within the events and purpose of his coming so near to us a baby. Did the infant Jesus warm her heart up to the miracle of what it would mean to the world when this baby grew up?

The next time we are drawn to hold or smile at a newborn baby, let us hear God's invitation: all who are weary and burdened, all who think our Lord is unapproachable, look again. See in the baby and the Messiah how personal, tangible, and approachable God's love truly is. Let's ponder, let's be amazed again, as Mary was: we can know God personally because he came as a baby, as one of us.

SHARE

Read and then discuss the question or questions that are best suited for the age of your child(ren).

1. Go to the Nativity set and look at the crib of baby Jesus. Then show your family and children a picture of a baby you all know. Ask: *Why do people like babies? What are some specific ways Jesus is just like a baby we know?*

2. Babies are so innocent and approachable. Christ, too, even grown up, was also very approachable! Yet many people believe God is unapproachable, distant, maybe even mad at them. Ask: *Who is someone in our extended family, neighborhood, school, or workplace that you think sees God like this? Why do you think he/she might believe God is like that?*

3. Go to the Nativity set and look at the crib and the shepherds and the Wise Men (or Magi). Baby Jesus got a lot of attention from his parents and all his visitors. Ask: *What is one way we like to pay attention to the baby Jesus during the Christmas season? What about during the rest of the year?*

SING

What Child is This?

What child is this, who, laid to rest,
On Mary's lap is sleeping?
Whom angels greet with anthems sweet,
While shepherds watch are keeping?

(Chorus) This, this is Christ the King,
Whom shepherds guard and angels sing.
Haste, haste to bring Him laud,
The babe, the Son of Mary.

PRAY

Father God, when we pause again at the miracle of Christmas, we remember how amazing it is that you want us to approach you, and that you want to be in relationship with us. Jesus, thank you for coming as a baby and then growing up to do your important job of loving and saving us. Help me to understand more about the life you came to live. Amen.

Jesus Was Born into a Family

FOCUS

Just like people grow up with mothers and fathers, siblings, aunts, uncles, and grandparents, so did Jesus. He was part of a family, too.

READ

Matthew 1:1-17 is Jesus' family tree. Listen for names and people that are for some reason "out of place."

REFLECT

Is there an ornament on your tree that has a picture of a baby, or one that prompts a memory of a child, or came from a family vacation memory? If so, let them be a reminder of something we all have in common with Jesus: a family and a heritage.

The genealogy in Matthew (also in Luke 3) makes it clear that Jesus came not only from God, but also from a family line. Jesus, the Son of God, was also the son of Joseph and Mary. His conception was unique, but his home life was rather normal; he grew up with parents and siblings, and perhaps his grandparents lived next door. Mary, like any mother, rocked her baby, showed him how to walk, and taught him good table manners. Joseph taught his son a trade and how to treat his little brothers and his village elders.

In addition, Joseph and Mary had normal extended families. Jesus had an Aunt Elizabeth and Cousin John (the Baptist), as well as a long line of ancestors. Listed in his family tree are heroes and harlots, princes and outsiders, and ordinary rescued failures like you and me. The genealogy of Jesus invites us to remember the biological generations that preceded us but also our spiritual heritage: we are now part of Christ's lineage, because everyone who approaches God with the simple faith of a child is welcome to join his family.

God placed his utmost trust in Mary and Joseph to care for his beloved son. Because Jesus was conceived by God's Spirit, Joseph made the conscious choice to call Jesus his own son. And because Jesus grew up in a home without his true, heavenly father, in a sense he was an "adopted" child. He experienced life in a family that was not fully his own; and like any adopted child, was not loved less for it, but perhaps more.

It is no accident that we who are made in the image of Jesus are given the privileged title of being God's adopted children. In Christ, we are adopted in God's family line with all the privileges of His inheritance here and now. God's Spirit bears witness that we are God's first choice.

"See what great a love the Father has bestowed on us that we should be called the children of God, and such we are." – 1 John 3:1

SHARE

Read and then discuss the question or questions that are best suited for the age of your child(ren).

1. Look at some pictures of your immediate family and your relatives. Have parents or kids retell a story or memory of their grandparents or great-grandparents.

2. Ask: *what are several examples of how our family has been important to us this last year?*

3. Consider how Jesus defined his family as anyone who obeys and follows him (Mark 3:35). Ask: *who is someone apart from our family that follows Jesus and feels like family?* (Remember, our brothers and sisters in Christ really are family!)

4. If any of your family members are adopted (or foster, etc.), include their heritage as a part of your family storytelling. Remember the story of how they became a part of your family.

SING

It Came upon a Midnight Clear

It came upon a midnight clear,
That glorious song of old,
From angels bending near the Earth,
With news of joy foretold,
"Peace on the Earth, goodwill to men
From Heavens all gracious King!"
The world in solemn stillness lay
To hear the angels sing.

PRAY

Dear Jesus, thank you for having a family, even an imperfect one, just like we do. You know what it's like to be a son and a sibling and have a heritage, just like we do. Thank you that you can be part of any family that welcomes you. Jesus, we welcome you into our family again this Christmas. Amen.

Jesus Was Born in a Special Place

FOCUS

Ornaments can come from special places. Our ornaments and the nativity set remind us that baby Jesus was also born in a special place.

READ

Open to **Luke 2:1-4 and Matthew 2:6, 13- 14.** Read and identify together as many places mentioned as you can.

REFLECT

Read through the Luke and Matthew Christmas stories above with an eye for places and you will quickly realize that Jesus' coming here involved many specific locations:

- The entire **Roman Empire** where the census was taken;

- **Israel**, the country where Jesus spent almost all of his life and ministry;

- **Nazareth**, Mary and Joseph's hometown;

- **Bethlehem**, its hillside home and stable, the location of the manger;

- **Egypt**, where his parents took him to find safety until the wicked king Herod died.

Conclusion? You can't separate the events of the Christmas drama from its sets and locations. Jesus' birthplace matters because place always matters to God.

Christ's birth and incarnation remind us all to see the ordinary places in our lives as important. Trailheads and tall buildings, parks and playgrounds, family rooms and boardrooms all matter to God. Everyone in our community flourishes best when we take seriously God's presence in the places where we live and work.

Jesus was called to a small patch of ground in the region of Nazareth, in Palestine. Do you remember what Jesus' contemporaries said about his hometown? They asked, "Can anything good come out of Nazareth?" Christ has a habit of showing up in the most unlikely of places.

Similarly, Jesus's coming to Earth calls us to put roots of active love in overlooked and otherwise seemingly insignificant places.

These little "patches" we live on are holy ground. What if we were to look for, love, and live for him there?

SHARE

Read and then discuss the question or questions that are best suited for the age of your child(ren).

1. Point out some of the tree's ornaments that came from a special place your family has experienced: a vacation, a road trip, a previous home, etc. Remember together a few stories about these places and what made those places special to you.

2. Describe, or better yet, find some pictures for your kids of a traditional Bethlehem cave on the internet. Ask: *How would you describe the special place that Jesus was born? Was it in a hospital or in a house? Was it a big or a little place? Was it amazing or ordinary?*

3. Use your "informed imagination," or look online for pictures or paintings of Jesus' Bethlehem, and of the city of Bethlehem today. Ask: *What does it tell us about God that he chose his Son to be born in this ordinary, out of the way, otherwise unremarkable place? What does it tell us about Jesus himself?*

SING

O Little Town of Bethlehem

O little town of Bethlehem,
How still we see thee lie,
Above thy deep and dreamless sleep
The silent stars go by.
Yet in thy dark streets shineth
The everlasting Light,
The hopes and fears of all the years
Are met in thee tonight.

PRAY

Dear Jesus, thank you for coming as a baby to do your important job of loving and saving us right here on Earth. Help me to understand through the ornaments and our Nativity set that you and I both were born in a special place. Jesus, because you are still alive and present everywhere, that means every place is important to you. Use us all, Lord, as your hands and feet where we are, wherever you have placed us. Amen.

Jesus Was Born at a Special Time

FOCUS

God chose a special time to send baby Jesus to Earth. Our time here on Earth is also special to Jesus and should be special to us!

READ

As you read **Luke 2:1-11**, emphasize the direct and indirect references to time. See if you can identify at least four (for example, "suddenly").

REFLECT

Many historians believe that Jesus was born in or around 4 BC. This was a time in history filled with violence, suffering, and crisis. The Roman Empire ruled much of the known world and taxation laid a heavy burden on all the people. Israel's local leader, Herod, kept control through violence and instilling great fear. It was a desperate time. After centuries of human oppression and God's silence, the Jews longed deeply for a Messiah to bring comfort and relief.

Jesus came at a unique and strategic time in world history. During previous centuries, the Romans had built a fine network of roads for their armies that stretched over much of their empire; little did they know that these same roads would also be used to spread the gospel across the known world. Their policing of thieves and other dangerous people on these roads and the seas also made safe travel feasible for the first time. Postal routes, a solid system of law and courts, and Greek as the common language throughout the empire—all these together helped the good news of Jesus spread far and wide.

It was no coincidence that the gospel and Paul's epistles spread so quickly after Jesus' death.

The Old Testament prophets had spoken of a time when the Messiah would come. No wonder the opening line in one of Jesus' first sermons was, "The time is fulfilled" (Mark 1:15). His words brimmed with meaning and caused a stirring of hope in the people.

We, too, live in a time of both danger and opportunity, a time where the world seems in crisis but is also poised for a rapid explosion of good in the coming kingdom of God. The world is linked together like never before, both by the internet and technology, and also by our interdependency. For example, a crop failure in one country can lead to a food shortage in another.

God has prepared us for such a time as this. He is present to us in every moment, minute, and hour. May God weave his divine purpose into our hours and days and stories here on Earth.

SHARE

Read and then discuss the question or questions that are best suited for the age of your child(ren).

1. Find several ornaments on your tree that have a specific event or year associated with them. Have someone who knows their significance share the dates and importance of these ornaments.

2. Remember together some special family memories or events from this year. Briefly retell a few of these stories.

3. Discuss some important happenings in your city, country, or world this year.

SING

It Came Upon a Midnight Clear

It came upon a midnight clear,
That glorious song of old,
From angels bending near the Earth,
With news of joy foretold,
"Peace on the Earth, goodwill to men
From Heavens all gracious King!"
The world in solemn stillness lay
To hear the angels sing.

PRAY

Dear Jesus, thank you for coming and using your time on Earth to do your important job of loving and saving us. Thank you for our ornaments and Nativity that remind us that you and I both were born at a special time in history. You are still a central part of our lives. Thank you that you will always be with us, no matter how many years go by. Amen.

Jesus Was Born a Hebrew

FOCUS

Jesus came to Earth in a human body, and not just any body, but the body of a Hebrew man. He looked like all of his Jewish neighbors. However, this doesn't mean Jesus loves just Jewish people, all cultures and ethnicities are welcome in his family.

READ

Find out more in **Isaiah 11:1 and Matthew 2:1-2**

REFLECT

Jesus was not blond and blue-eyed as some Sunday school portraits might suggest. As a Jewish man, he would have had dark hair, dark eyes, and Hebrew features. His family tree was of the house of David and the line of Jesse (Isaiah 11:1).

Christ's Jewish heritage reminds us that our native cultures are not irrelevant to God; rather, our culture is an integral part of our human story as it was in Jesus. We swim in a sea of our culture's values, practices, norms, traditions, stories, and symbols. Our culture, created by both God and humans, cannot be separated from who we are. Nor can we pretend these aspects of our life don't exist or matter. We should understand and explore our own cultural heritage, appreciating and, whenever possible, conforming it to the character of Jesus Christ.

While culture is a gift, we must also be careful not to mold God into our own cultural likeness. Ancient gods and religious values were often created from idealized humans, and the Christian faith has done the same thing. It has been said, "God made Adam and Eve in his image, and then they returned the favor." Even though Jesus came from a Middle Eastern culture, many people still tend to recreate him into a person who not only looks like they do, but thinks and acts like they do, too.

It's so easy to take all this one step further and only associate with those who are familiar to us and those who look like us. If we fall into this trap, we miss the beauty of God's diversity.

All this helps us see why God called the Magi from a different culture to be the first non-Bethlehem visitors to see and worship baby Jesus. Their message rings out: Jesus coming as a Hebrew does not make Jesus exclusive to one ethnicity; rather, Jesus gives value and welcomes every culture. All nations and peoples were welcomed at his birth and will be found at Jesus' throne in Heaven (Revelation 7:9-10).

No wonder Matthew's gospel ends with Christ's capstone teaching to the early church to "make disciples of all nations, *tribes, and cultures*" (Matthew 28:19).

SHARE

Read and then discuss the question or questions that are best suited for the age of your child(ren).

1. Look at the three Magi in your Nativity set and remember that they came from far away. Ask: *How might they have been looked at and welcomed by the local people?*

2. Find a picture on the internet of a Middle Eastern man, and then ask your family to imagine Jesus with these features. Ask: *Is this picture different from other pictures you have seen of Jesus?*

3. We know it matters a great deal to God that people from other subcultures in our city hear about Jesus. Together, pick one group of people in your city that you believe Jesus cares about and pray for them.

SING

O Come, O Come, Emmanuel

O come, O come, Emmanuel
And ransom captive Israel,
That mourns in lonely exile here
Until the Son of God appear.
Rejoice! Rejoice! Emmanuel
Shall come to Thee, O Israel.

PRAY

Dear Jesus, thank you for coming as a Hebrew, but for also wanting to welcome every nation, every culture, and every land in your important work of loving the whole world. Help us embrace the gifts of different races and cultures. Send your people past our own familiar people and places to the very ends of the Earth (Acts 1:8).

Jesus Was Born into Hardship

FOCUS

The songs and images of Christmas, both Christian and secular, tend to make the manger scene "merry and bright," full of peace and joy. Jesus, however, experienced both poverty and persecution in his birth and life. That's good news for those who experience the same today.

READ

Read and think about **Matthew 2:13-18 and Corinthians 8:9**

REFLECT

Signs of poverty are well known parts of the Christmas story. Jesus shared his birth room with the family's animals, and it was a stone manger that held him first. Socially looked down upon, shepherds served as his unlikely first visitors. When eight days later Jesus was circumcised, his parents could only afford a turtledove for their temple sacrifice.

Persecution and murder are also a tragic part of his birth story. In attempting to find and snuff out the Christ child, Herod ordered that all the baby boys of Bethlehem two years and under be killed. The grief and agony of their mothers and fathers filled the city. Jesus' family was forced to become refugees, fleeing to Egypt in fear for their lives.

His beginnings were anything but all "merry and bright," full of silence and peace. Hardship continued to surround him well beyond Bethlehem.

Jesus grew up in a small home and a small village both occupied and heavily taxed by the Romans. Life for the majority was hand-to-mouth. As an adult, Jesus lived without having a house or money saved in an account. He traveled from town to town with only the clothes on his back.

The unending military occupation placed a day in, day out heavy burden on everyone. If Roman soldiers entered a town, they could plunder its money, food, livestock, and other resources at will. Towns were poor and violence visited the people regularly, which is not unlike the regular experience of many people around the world.

Those of us who live in prosperity and religious freedom may easily overlook these harsh realities woven throughout the Christmas story. But for those living on the margins of society, Jesus' poverty and persecution come as good news. God chose the shepherds, who were familiar with poverty and social scorn, to be the first to find Jesus and Christmas joy.

Perhaps it's still true today, that those who can identify with the shame and suffering that Christ experienced are often the first ones to recognize him.

SHARE

Read and then discuss the question or questions that are best suited for the age of your child(ren).

1. Remember again several ways Jesus and his parents did not experience what they should have in the Christmas story. Ask: *Are there people who are poor like Jesus in our community? Who and where are they?* Pray as a family for the poor in your community.

2. Use a globe to help you pray for people in another part of the world who may be hungry, poor, or persecuted today. Remember that Jesus shared a similar experience.

3. Find on the internet a story of a persecuted Christian. Briefly discuss, then pray together.

SING

The First Noel

The first Noel the angels did sing
Was to certain poor shepherds in fields as they lay,

In fields where they lay keeping their sheep,
On a cold winter's night that was so deep.

(Chorus) Noel, Noel, Noel, Noel,
Born is the King of Israel!

PRAY

Father God, life was difficult for Jesus, Mary and Joseph. We thank you, Jesus, for loving us enough to come and become poor *like* us and poor *for* us. In doing so, we know you can relate to those who are poor and persecuted. Meet us all with hope in our hardships, Lord. Lead us away from the pursuit of a life without struggle. Help us to bring hope to others who suffer from poverty and persecution in our world. Amen

WE GIVE BECAUSE GOD GAVE FIRST

1. Watch *It's a Wonderful Life*, 1947. (Notice the theme of our life being a gift to the world.) Or, watch *Veggie Tales: The Toy that Saved Christmas*, 1996. (Note the theme that Christmas is not about getting gifts, but about giving, just as God gave us Jesus.)

2. Make a gift for someone you love outside of your family (a neighbor, teacher, or friend). This gift could be a card, a food item, a piece of art or a craft, or something you build or write. Or you could make a "coupon" to bake something, do a chore, babysit, or perform some other helpful service.

3. Read a suggested story from *The New Guideposts Christmas Treasury*, found in Appendix II.

We Give Because God Gave First

FOCUS

Our Christmas ifts remind us that the greatest gift we can receive is Jesus. When we receive the gift of Jesus from God, we naturally want to give gifts to others.

TRADITIONS AND ACTIVITIES

1. Take the baby Jesus from the Nativity set, wrap him in a box, and put him under the tree. As you do, remember, the starting place of Christmas is receiving the gift of Jesus.

2. Put up your stockings. Remember the legend of Santa Claus, as tradition has it, put gifts in socks that were hung to dry over the fireplace (see Reflect below).

3. Read **Luke 2: 8-18** as you light the third Advent candle, which is traditionally called the "Shepherd's Candle." The shepherds received the gift of the "good news" of Jesus' birth and then shared that gift to others. We are to do the same.

4. Wrap and put some presents under the tree. Remember that they are all a response to the gift of Jesus' coming.

REFLECT

The person of Santa Claus comes from the legend of Saint Nicholas, a bishop who lived centuries ago and who deeply loved God and people. He became famous for showing his gratitude to God by giving gifts to poor children in his city. Legend has it he left his gifts in the stockings people had laid by the hearth to dry overnight. His story has since captured the hearts of millions around the world; many nations practice a tradition of stockings and giving surprises and goodies to children on Christmas.

Saint Nicholas freely received from Christ, so freely he gave (Matt. 10:18). This same response of giving is wonderfully displayed in the first Christmas shepherds. Motivated by first seeing the Christ child with their own eyes, the shepherds eagerly spread the story of the angels' message to those around them. Proclaiming God's gift became their gift to the world.

However, it can be easy to forget that the foundation of our holiday giving is the extravagant coming of Christ. Even though we are Jesus' followers, we can still be tempted to just give presents because it's a custom or give with the hope of getting a gift in return. Deep down we know that we are to be motivated at Christmas by something deeper.

Here is the good news: What was true for Christ in one particular moment of history ends up being true forever and everywhere. This means that the everyday places and people of all cultures and epochs, the ordinary and sometimes dreary circumstances of life—all of these matter to God. That is why each follower of Jesus is one of God's special ornaments.

SING

Angels We Have Heard on High
Verse 2

Shepherds, why this jubilee?
Why your joyous strains prolong?
What the gladsome tidings be
Which inspire your heavenly song?

Angels we have heard on high
Sweetly singing o'er the plains,
And the mountains in reply
Echoing their joyous strains.

(Chorus) Gloria, in excelsis Deo! (x2)

PRAY

Thank You, God, for the greatest gift ever given, Your Son Jesus. Thank You, Jesus, that You came to save us and give us life. Father God, open our eyes more and more this Christmas to see the gift of our coming Savior. Jesus, may our Christmas presents and other gifts of love this year be our free and natural response to the gift of you. Amen.

Jesus Was a Surprise from God

FOCUS

No one was expecting Jesus to come to Earth when he did. He came like our Christmas gifts under the tree: all wrapped up as a surprise for the world!

READ

Jesus arrived and spoke to people's hearts in joyful surprise as you'll read in **Luke 2:7, 36-38**.

REFLECT

Today we explore one of the most referred to aspects of Jesus' birth: he was "wrapped in swaddling clothes." The Father first wrapped up his Son in a human form in Mary's womb; soon after he was born, she in turn wrapped baby Jesus in strips of cloth.

The practice of wrapping presents is such an important part of the Christmas gift experience, isn't it? How could young children have the same wild-eyed anticipation for Christmas if we simply laid our gifts bare at the base of the tree? The wrapping keeps us anticipating something new, a surprise that will bring us joy.

Surprise is no stranger to the Christmas story. Anna experienced her fair share of surprises, including the unexpected early death of her husband. After this tragedy, she decided to pass her days in the temple, praying, fasting, and watching for the appearance of God's Redeemer. When Joseph and Mary entered with baby Jesus, the voice of God spoke to her sensitive heart, saying, "This is the one."

The humility of God coming as a baby briefly surprised her, but it did not disappoint her. She shared the shocking good news with all who would listen.

In the end, Jesus' naked, unwrapped death on the cross was the largest surprise of all, but it was also history's grandest gift. In his Second Coming, Christ will again surprise us. His glory and his kingdom will catch us off guard in a way we can only begin to imagine.

As we wait for that day, God will continue to surprise us with his love, provision, and direction. May the Lord give us the joy of expectation as we wait for the next surprising gift our Christ will surely bring us.

SHARE

Read and then discuss the question or questions that are best suited for the age of your child(ren).

1. Grab a present under the tree that is "safe" to let a child shake. Try to guess what it is. Feel the anticipation that comes from not yet knowing what surprise awaits for the one who will open it.

2. Put a present under the tree from someone outside your immediate family. Imagine together how different Christmas would be if we did not wrap our gifts, or if they weren't a surprise. Ask: *Why do you, and why do most people, enjoy surprises?*

3. Ask: *What is something that happened this year that was unexpected...even something unexpected that originally appeared to be negative, but surprisingly, brought about something good?*

SING

Away in a Manger

Away in a manger, no crib for a bed,
The little Lord Jesus laid down his sweet head.
The stars in the sky looked down where He lay,
The little Lord Jesus asleep in the hay.

Be near me, Lord Jesus, I ask Thee to stay
Close by me forever, and love me, I pray.
Bless all the dear children in Thy tender care,
And take us to Heaven, to live with Thee there.

PRAY

Father God, thank you for surprising us with baby Jesus, who came to save us and give us life. Jesus, help us see that you still surprise us with your love and the way you come to us. Help us to live more like Anna, to wait for your timing and surrender our plans, so that we can be ready for your surprises in our everyday life. Amen.

Jesus' Gift Was a Sacrifice

FOCUS

Jesus sacrificed so much to save us, his flock, and He is still willing to do whatever it takes to rescue and love all his lost sheep. We, too, are sometimes called to sacrifice in order to help others.

READ

Turn to **Luke 15:3-7 and John 10:11** in your Bible.

REFLECT

In the original Christmas story, giving involved sacrifice. On the night the angels sang, God provided what Abraham had long ago believed God would provide on his altar: a sacrificial lamb to take Isaac's place (Genesis 22:8). In coming to Earth centuries later, Jesus temporarily emptied himself of heaven's honor to come as the Lamb of God who would take our place, too. His mission was to be Heaven's offering for Earth's salvation. It cost Jesus everything to come as the Lamb, to be the ultimate offering and sacrifice.

We must not miss here the example of the shepherds. The shepherds of the first Christmas were willing to leave their flocks vulnerable to predators in order to see for themselves the one who came "to seek and save the lost" (Luke 19:10). This risk-taking to find the baby, however, was not surprising. For the sake of their sheep, shepherds often had to put their lives in danger and worked long hours away from family.

Other characters in the Christmas story were also willing to experience sacrifice. Mary laid down her comfort, courtship with Joseph, and her reputation to carry baby Jesus in her virgin womb. Anna the prophetess long denied herself of a normal social life, fasting and praying for decades while she waited for the Messiah. The Magi lost valuable time away from their homes and gave costly treasures to the child.

Jesus' first gift of incarnation and second gift of death cost him everything. We can never match his extravagance, but in our own way, we can give something back. We are to offer sacrifices of love from what we have and who we are. Indeed, Paul in Romans 12:1 says that the sacrifice God wants from us is to offer up to him our bodies and our ordinary, everyday lives for his extraordinary purposes.

This life of sacrifice for others is costly, but always worth the reward. And in the end, we are simply giving back to God what is already his.

SHARE

Read and then discuss the question or questions that are best suited for the age of your child(ren).

1. Hang a number of red and white candy canes on the tree and/or serve hot cocoa, using a candy cane to stir it. Notice that the candy canes are shaped like a shepherd's staff to remind us that Jesus was and is our Good Shepherd. He made great sacrifices to love and find us. You can also share with your kids how the red stripes on the candy cane represent our sin; the white stripes symbolize the pure, sinless nature of the Lamb of God who came to shed his blood for us.

2. Ask your children to talk about an experience where they lost something that took a lot of effort and time to find. Ask: *how did you feel when you finally found what you were searching for?*

3. Have one person retell a situation from the last year where either he/she did or received something for another person that involved some level of sacrifice? Ask: *how did the experience of sacrifice make you feel?*

SING

Joy to the World

Joy to the World, the Lord is come!
Let earth receive her King;
Let every heart prepare Him room,
And Heaven and nature sing. (x3)

PRAY

Thank you, Jesus, our Good Shepherd, for laying down your life for us. Thank you for the sacrifices you have made for us, your sheep. Lord, it's not easy to put the needs of others before our own. Help us to be willing to sacrifice for the people you want us to love. Amen.

God's Gifts Come Without Expectation

FOCUS

Just like Saint Nicholas gave presents, God gave Jesus to us even though we could not give him something in return. We, too, are to give presents freely with no strings attached.

READ

Gather and read **Luke 6:32-33 and Matthew 25:35-40** in your Bible.

REFLECT

The holiday traditions we find across the globe of giving and receiving presents can all be traced back to Saint Nicholas, who secretly gave gifts to the poor, to those who could not give a present back to him.

Christmas presents today, however, are usually not one-way gifts like Saint Nicholas' were. Instead they are often given in an exchange. Our traditions with family, coworkers, neighbors, or friends usually follow the unspoken pattern: "I give you something and you give me something." That kind of giving is normal, easy, and predictable.

However, God's gift of Jesus was given with no expectation that we could ever give something equal in return. What gift of ours could ever compare to his Son, who is both innocent baby and King of kings? Any response or gift we could offer falls embarrassingly short of his extravagance toward us.

Even though we may fail to respond to his love, or even realize it's there, God's giving keeps coming. Our response does not affect his faithfulness. Christ made it clear: we can never love God the way he loves us. However, Christ offered us another channel for expressing our love to him—that is, loving the thirsty, the hungry, and the stranger among us, is mysteriously loving him.

Perhaps that is why millions of people at Christmas, many without knowing what they are fully doing, find ways to serve and give to those who cannot give an equal gift in return. When we do, we actually receive precious but intangible gifts in our heart that cannot be bought at any store.

Let the Magi be our example of how we can love as Jesus taught us. They laid their treasures at the feet of Mary and Joseph, and the newborn baby, the peasant family who could not afford to give anything in return. In doing so, they were loving God himself.

May God lead us this Christmas, and all year long, to love those in our family, neighborhood, and community without expectation that they give us something back.

SHARE

Read and then discuss the question or questions that are best suited for the age of your child(ren).

1. Put together a simple and anonymous Christmas gift for a neighbor who is not expecting it or who will not know how to give back to you. Leave this gift on their doorstep. Come back home and briefly share together about the experience.

2. Talk together about some ways that people in your community give to those who can't give back during the holiday season. (Maybe a local business has a giving tree that your kids have noticed or there are Gospel Mission bell ringers at your grocery store.)

3. Share a time when you were sick or hurt, and someone offered an act of love that you could not readily reciprocate. Ask: *what did this experience make you feel or think?*

SING

O Come All Ye Faithful

O come, all ye faithful,
Joyful and triumphant,
O come ye, O come ye to Bethlehem.
Come and behold Him,
Born the King of Angels.

(Chorus) O come, let us adore Him, (x3)
Christ the Lord.

PRAY

Father God, you are generous. You gave us the gift of Jesus to save us and give us life, even though we could never give back to you a gift of equal value. Help us at Christmas and all year long to give to those who cannot give back to us. Make us most content when we are least recognized for what we do and give. Amen.

Worship, Thanks, and Praise Are Our Gifts to God

FOCUS

When Mary found out she was pregnant with baby Jesus, she gave thanks to God. When we, like Mary, thank God for who he is and what he has done for us, God's heart fills with joy.

READ

Mary had a song in her heart that glorified the Lord. Read **Luke 1:46-49; Matthew 2:1-2, 10-11.**

REFLECT

Moments of worship dot the entire landscape of the Christmas story. It started with a baby in Elizabeth's womb who leapt for joy in Jesus' presence. Elizabeth realized she was in the presence of the Holy One and began to praise her cousin. Mary quickly made sure Elizabeth understood that any admiration should not be for her: "My soul magnifies the Lord and my spirit exalts my God." Her prayer, called the Magnificat, is pure adoration that also highlights the plight of the poor.

Another significant example of worship is the choir of angels who were "heard on high" when they came out in the evening sky and surprised the shepherds. Their message is overflowing with joy and praise: the baby the shepherds will find is no-run-of-the-mill Messiah pretender. He is the Lord! What good the Savior will bring to Earth!

The Magi made the clearest connection between worship and gift-giving. Believing the star would lead them to a great earthly king, they brought the costliest gifts from the ancient Near East: gold, frankincense, and myrrh.

The root word for worship in English is "worthy." To the Magi, the newborn king was worthy of their worship and most treasured gifts. Jesus' character makes him rightfully worthy of our adoration, not only in our church buildings, but also in our classrooms, living rooms, bedrooms and boardrooms.

Anywhere we are, Jesus is worthy of our worship.

When we seek to offer each moment and word and action to God, we become an offering in his sight. Our love, kindness, and justice translate in God's presence to the words "we thank you" and "we praise you."

This is the daily worship God wants us to offer.

May we bring our precious gift of worship to the King all year long!

SHARE

Read and then discuss the question or questions that are best suited for the age of your child(ren).

1. Have parents share a gift they see in each of the kids they are thankful for, then end with praising God for being the source of these gifts.

2. Have one or more share a time this year when someone appreciated or said something nice about them. Ask: *how did that make them feel?* In light of these, remind yourselves how our worship and thanks to God makes him feel.

3. Put some money on the table. It's one thing people feel is valuable enough to revolve their lives around making and spending. Ask: *what other things or beliefs do people in our culture value and "worship" more than God?*

SING

Angels We Have Heard On High

Angels we have heard on high
Sweetly singing o'er the plains,
And the mountains in reply
Echoing their joyous strains.

(Chorus) Gloria, in excelsis Deo! (x2)

Come to Bethlehem and see
him Whose birth the angels sing;
Come, adore on bended knee,
Christ the Lord, the newborn King.

PRAY

Great and extravagant God, you gave to us your most valuable gift, your son Jesus. For this gift of immeasurable worth, we worship and thank you. Keep us from the temptation to value anything more than you. May we in our life choices worship and value you above everything else. Amen.

God Gave Us Gifts to Share

FOCUS

The Magi used their gifts of knowing the stars to find their way to baby Jesus and offer him their treasures. We also can be a gift to other people when we share our special and unique talents with them.

READ

Read what Paul has to say about spiritual gifts in **1 Corinthians 12:4-6, 27.**

REFLECT

In the classic Christmas story "The Little Drummer Boy," the young orphan brought to the Bethlehem stable a special gift, a gift that couldn't be bought at a store or even wrapped in a box. Instead, the little boy played his drum. This gift of humble playing, offered in faith, blessed everyone who heard him. A sense of holy magic filled the air. Even the baby Jesus was pleased.

Like the young drummer, others in the Christmas story also gave their simple, God-given talents. The Wise Men used their knowledge of the stars to successfully make the trip from their homeland to Bethlehem. Anna exercised her passion to pray. Simeon used his gift of prophecy to help him recognize the baby as the Messiah. Without these gifts being used or offered, the Christmas story would not read the same.

God created each of us with a unique personality and special ways to love others. The Bible appropriately calls these "gifts." When we are true to who we really are, we use our gifts on behalf of others, not simply for ourselves. In the process, the ones we love, and God himself, experience our very lives as a gift.

Therefore, recognize and rejoice in how God designed you with abilities that can bless others. You are God's masterpiece and you fill an essential role in God's family. This coming year, dive further into the journey of knowing the gift God calls "you." Discover how your gifts help you serve God and others. Find your important place in the body of Christ.

When we all do this, the arms and legs and every other part of Christ's Body, the Church, work together. Touched by our gifts, the world experiences through us the goodness and love of God.

SHARE

Read and then discuss the question or questions that are best suited for the age of your child(ren).

1. Ask: *what is one way our family used a talent or ability God gave us to love someone else?* (Parents can start or tell the whole story.)

2. Ask: *what is one gift or ability you see in yourself that you used somehow to bless or love someone else this last year?* Give everyone a piece of paper and have them write their names on the top. Then, pass the papers around so that everyone can write down a talent or a gift they see in that person. When finished, have each person read aloud what is written on his or her own paper.

3. Tonight would be a good night to do Sunday's **Connect to Others** suggestion.

SING

Little Drummer Boy

Come they told me, pa rum pum pum pum,
A new born king to see, pa rum pum pum pum,
Our finest gifts we bring, pa rum pum pum pum,
To lay before the king, pa rum pum pum pum,
Rum pum pum pum (x2)
So to honor him, pa rum pum pum pum,
When we come.

PRAY

Offer your own group prayer to God today. Thank God for one or more specific blessings your family has received this year through the shared resources or talents of others. Then, thank him for a specific ability or talent he has given to you to use to live and love others well. Feel God's delight in you and your family.

My Yes Is a Gift to God

FOCUS

When God in Heaven asked Jesus to do his important job on Earth, Jesus said *yes*. When the angel asked Mary to do her important job of being Jesus' mother, Mary said *yes*. It's a gift to God when we say yes to his leading.

READ

To read of Mary's "yes" open to **Luke 1:30-38.**

REFLECT

Mary stands out in the Christmas story as the first person to receive Jesus and give back to him. In her miraculous conception, Mary received the gift of God in the most personal way possible: in her own body. The angel's announcement filled Mary's heart with questions and fear, yet her simple response reveals her gift back to God: "I am willing to be used by the Lord" (Luke 1:38, paraphrased).

Despite the certain backlash of rumors that would certainly come, Mary gave God her best *yes*. She welcomed the baby Christ to develop and grow in her through the Holy Spirit. Her gift to God was simply her availability and her continual *yes* to the miracle baby growing within her.

Isn't she an inspiration to all of us?

Mary, a simple virgin girl, favored by God, refused to let fear determine her decision. She allowed the love of God to take full sway in her heart and body. In her beautiful gift of surrender, she added the posture of humility to the virtue of availability: "Behold your bondservant. Let it be done to me, Lord, as you have said" (Luke 1:38).

God wants us all to say *yes* to his leading in how we handle our time, money, words, and relationships. Letting God always be the leader is the hard work of surrender. For example, thinking of time and money as "our" time and "our" money reveals the root issue: we like to be in control more than we like to let go. It can be dreadfully hard to let go of our own human plans, to simply believe that God loves us, and to respond with a consistent *yes* to his leading.

Lord, help us in our decisions small and big, to believe, and to say *yes* as Mary did.

SHARE

Read and then discuss the question or questions that are best suited for the age of your child(ren).

1. Write ahead of time the words "Yes, Lord" and the names of each family member on a piece of colored paper. Show it to everyone, then wrap it up in a small box and put it under the tree. This gift represents your family's willingness to say yes to God.

2. Ask your kids to make a "coupon" for one other person in the family to do a chore in the week ahead (for example, cleaning the toilet, sweeping the porch). Remind them that when the coupon is redeemed, they can show obedience to God by being quick to say *yes*.

3. Consider the important job the angel asked Mary to do. Ask: *what would have made it hard for Mary to say yes? Think about this last year—was there a time when you perhaps related to Mary, where it was hard for you to say yes to what you knew God wanted you to do?*

SING

O Little Town of Bethlehem
Verse 3

How silently, how silently
The wondrous gift is given!
So God imparts to human hearts
The blessings of His Heaven.
No ear may hear His coming,
But in this world of sin,
Where meek souls will receive Him still,
The dear Christ enters in.

PRAY

Thank you, God, for the greatest gift ever given, Jesus your son. He said *yes* to coming to Earth as a baby, *yes* to loving us so well, *yes* to dying on the cross and rising from the dead. Thank you for Mary, too, who also said *yes* when you gave her a challenging job! We say *yes* to you using us to spread your love and light wherever we go, in whatever we do. Yes! Amen.

THE STAR AND ANGELS POINT TO JESUS

1. Watch *Rudolph the Red-Nosed Reindeer, 1964*. (Rudolph's red nose guides Santa like the Christmas star guided the Wise Men.)
   Or, watch *A Christmas Carol* (pay attention to how the three spirits act as guides, as "stars," to help Scrooge find the truth).
   Or, watch *The Polar Express, 2004*. (Watch the theme unfold of how it takes the gift of faith to believe.)

2. Share one person from your family, school, workplace, or neighborhood who needs someone to point them to Jesus. Pray for them today by name.

3. Read a suggested story from *The New Guideposts Christmas Treasury*, found in Appendix II.

The Star and Angels Point to Jesus

FOCUS

God used stars and angels to guide the Wise Men and the shepherds to find the baby Jesus. The story's stars and angels remind us that we, too, sometimes need someone to guide us and help us find Jesus in our lives.

TRADITIONS AND ACTIVITIES

1. Put up your star or angel at the top of your tree.

2. Hang an angel ornament(s) on your Christmas tree, mantel, or on a shelf. If you have already put up your star and angel decorations, point them out to everyone.

3. Light the fourth Advent candle, the "Star Candle." Read **Matthew 2:1-2, 10-11 and Luke 2:8-14.** As you do, consider acting out one or both of these Bible passages as a family. The children (the shepherds and Wise Men) can follow a parent or older child carrying a flashlight (representing the star and the angels) around the house to "find" the baby Jesus. Even if you don't act out the passages, watch and listen for how the star and angels helped the characters find Jesus.

REFLECT

The Magi lived in a time when people looked to the stars for answers. They trusted them enough that when a unique star appeared in the east, the Magi traveled hundreds of miles to follow it and understand its mystery. When they arrived in Israel, they did not know exactly where God's divine gift would be found. They first stopped and asked for help in Jerusalem, Israel's more important city and historic capital. The priests in Herod's court shared the location where their Messiah should appear: "In Bethlehem of Judea."

These Eastern experts of the stars would have been shocked: why would the Ruler of the Universe be found here in this obscure town or make his entry into their world as a poor baby boy? The Magi—like all of us—would never have discovered Jesus on their own. They needed help to get past their own misperceptions of how a king should look and be born.

But the Magi were not the only ones who required assistance to see clearly.

Angels had to tell Mary and Joseph about the divine conception, the baby's destiny, and their need to flee to Egypt. The shepherds had help too.

Centuries later, we still need help to overcome our misperceptions that often blind us to the truth (Isaiah 9:2). Personal speculation alone cannot lead us to find Jesus.

Here is the good news: the God who sent angels that first Christmas still wants to help all people to find and delight in his Son. God no longer uses stars but rather his indwelling Holy Spirit and other people to point us to Jesus. The mission of the Christmas star and angels has become ours as well: we point a waiting world to the One who can still bring a new hope to the human heart (John 15:26). And when one of the lost discovers their place in God's family, the angels still rejoice.

SING

Hark the Herald Angels Sing

Hark the herald angels sing,
"Glory to the newborn King!
Peace on Earth and mercy mild
God and sinners reconciled."
Joyful, all ye nations rise
Join the triumph of the skies
With angelic host proclaim,
"Christ is born in Bethlehem."
(Repeat the first two lines above).

PRAY

Thank you, Lord, for sending the star and the angels so people could find the new baby Jesus. Thank you, too, for the family, friends, and circumstances that act like the angel and stars to guide us to you and the truth. Lord, when we see others still lost, others who have never looked up and seen your star or heard angel's voices, may we be like stars pointing them to you. Amen.

73

The Star Points to a Greater Christmas

FOCUS

As wonderful as the Wise Men's worship and the shepherds' joy were in the first Coming of Christ, they cannot compare with the joy and worship we will experience in the second and more dramatic coming of Christ. The first Christmas is just a rehearsal for the future coming of Jesus.

READ

Isaiah 60:1, 3, 6 describe what other kings and Wise Men will do when Jesus comes to Earth the second time.

REFLECT

"Advent," which means "the coming," helps us remember and celebrate the first and the Second Coming of Jesus. Before Jesus was born, the Israelites had waited a long time for the first appearance of their Messiah. God's people today wait for the return of Christ their victorious Lord.

Scripture tells us that Jesus' Second Coming will be on a much larger scale than what happened at Bethlehem. The star of God's overwhelming glory will replace the Magi's original star (Isaiah 60). It will seem as if all the stars have moved so close to Earth that we will need to turn away and cover our eyes. This time, no one will miss his coming and its good news; everyone will know that God is truly with us as King over all the Earth.

When my wife Carissa and I were living near Bethlehem in 1992, we decided to visit the church of the Nativity without a tour guide. Joined by two friends, we snuck past the attendants and found the stairway to the tower. From there, we could look north to see the traditional site of the field where the angels first appeared to the shepherds "watching their flocks by night" (Luke 2:8).

As we began to sing "O Little town of Bethlehem" and other traditional Christmas songs, our thoughts were flooded with the biblical story of Christ's first coming. I then found myself imagining my new Palestinian Christian friends singing by my side. I turned around and looked to see the shops of those living here now, the tourist shops we had visited, remembering their stories of oppression and hopelessness under the oppression of both their Muslim neighbors and the Israeli government.

I realized that for my Bethlehem sisters and brothers, Christmas had to be about more than Christ's first coming if it was to bring joy and truly good news. The first coming of Jesus to Bethlehem had brought them tourists and business, but no hope. Without the Christmas hope of his second coming, the words of all the cherished carols we were singing somehow felt hollow and incomplete.

It was here, in this Bethlehem bell tower, that I learned that Jesus' birth is only the beginning of the Christmas story. A greater Christmas will come, bringing a final end to injustice and suffering. And knowing this, I found my voice again in that bell tower. Even today, I can imagine singing Christmas carols there with Palestinian and persecuted Christians declaring our hope to the world.

SHARE

1. Set the table for your next meal (even if a day early) together as a family. As you do, remember that when Jesus comes again everyone will be welcome. Everyone who loves Jesus will gather around the bigger table of Heaven's incredible feast. Imagine together what Heaven's feast will be like.

SING

Joy to the World

Joy to the World, the Lord is come!
Let earth receive her King;
Let every heart prepare Him room,
And Heaven and nature sing. (x3)

No more let sins and sorrows grow,
Nor thorns infest the ground;
He comes to make His blessings flow
Far as the curse is found. (x3)

PRAY

Father God, you promise that a final day is coming when Jesus, the "Star of Glory," will reappear. When that second Christmas comes, dictators and rulers who commit injustices will be reduced to nothing. Princes will acknowledge that Jesus Christ is the true King. Every tear will melt away forever. Thank you Lord for your promised future that will far surpass the joy and worship of the first shepherds and Wise Men. Amen.

The Angels Point to the Future

FOCUS

The angels directed the shepherds to the physical location of baby Jesus, but they were also pointing to a future day when Jesus would bring "peace on Earth" and make the world perfect again.

READ

John is given a view of the New Heaven and New Earth in **Revelation 21:1-7, 22:1-5.**

REFLECT

The shepherds, along with all the Jewish people, were waiting for a future king to come and reign and return life on Earth to God's original plan. They, too, lived under the burden of their Roman oppressors and longed for freedom. The angels came announcing "peace and goodwill" for all people, a peace that would start in Bethlehem with Jesus but would only come to its fullness in his Second Coming.

Christmas points to a future when Christ will come again and have victory over sin and death, and make all things new. Knowing the end of the story can change the way we can live our lives here and now in difficult situations.

At the end of World War II, in a Nazi prisoner camp in the heart of Germany, Allied prisoners endured a daily life of drudgery, despair, and suffering. A change in their dire circumstances seemed impossible. However, when they secretly acquired a shortwave radio, the prisoners experienced a change in perspective -even joy. With this small box, they were able to establish contact with the outside world and gather true information about the war.

One day, the radio declared the jubilant news that Germany had surrendered. The message that the war was finally over spread quickly and led to dancing, hugs, and even smiling at the German guards. The previous hardships of their imprisonment now felt lighter. Days later, the guards received the same news and quietly slipped away, leaving the prison doors open. At last, they were free from bondage.

During the final days of captivity, these prisoners had a secret joy in their routine of drudgery, because they knew that the enemy had been defeated and their time in chains was ending soon. Justice had won even if their captors still seemed to be in control.

The angels in the Christmas story were like the radio in the story. They proclaimed the good news that Jesus himself would soon bring a hope-filled future kingdom to those who felt oppressed and even abandoned by God. Perhaps one of those same Bethlehem angels shared with the Apostle John the more detailed Revelation 21-22 vision of the future new Heaven and Earth. These two angelic proclamations bring us good news about the future. Knowing the story will end with a bright, victorious day can help those who live in the "prison of pain" live with joy and courage.

SHARE

Read and then discuss the question or questions that are best suited for the age of your child(ren).

1. Ask: *name several things that will be different in the world when Jesus comes to make everything perfect, loving, and good.*

2. Describe together one major problem going on in the world right now. Then imagine how this situation will change when Jesus brings his peace and love fully to Earth.

3. The descriptions and symbols of Revelation 21-22 reveal what will happen when Jesus comes again to bring Heaven to Earth. Ask: *what will this new reality mean for life on Earth? What will change and be different in our relationship with God or with each other?*

SING

Joy to the World

Joy to the World, the Lord is come!
Let earth receive her King;
Let every heart prepare him room,
And Heaven and nature sing. (x3)

Joy to the World, the Savior reigns!
Let men their songs employ;
While fields and floods, rocks, hills and plains
Repeat the sounding joy. (x3)

PRAY

Lord, help us to remember the future you have promised us when Jesus comes again. Like the angels, help us point people in our families, schools, neighborhoods, and workplaces to the hope that one day you will return to make everything right again. Amen.

Jesus Is the Star We Truly Seek

FOCUS

People throughout the ages have desired to have a leader or a hero to bring hope and direction to the challenges of their times. So we wait. We look for such a "star," and are often disappointed. But Jesus grew up to become that promised Star that can now guide the whole world to truth and God.

READ

Read **Numbers 24:15-17 and Revelation 22:16.**

REFLECT

Have you ever heard the Bible story about the donkey that talked to Balaam? (See **Numbers 22:21-39** if you want to read that story.) This mysterious man was sent from the eastern country of Moab to the desert by a king called Balak. He ordered Balaam to go into the desert, find the encampment of the people of Israel, and curse them. Instead, upon arriving at a lookout location, Balaam locked his eyes on the twelve tribes and blessed Israel—not just once, but twice! (Numbers 24:3-9)

At the end of his mission, Balaam was so impressed by Israel and inspired by their God that he spoke a prophecy: one day a star will come out of Jacob. This star will rule and lead God's people to crush her enemies. (Numbers 24:17)

Not surprisingly, future Hebrew generations found an anchor of hope in Balaam's prediction of a new and future star. Some devoted religious people, called the Essenes, who lived in the desert near Jerusalem, interpreted this star prophecy to mean a strong, heroic king who, with mighty warriors, would come and set them free from their Roman captors.

But they were disappointed. The Messiah they were waiting for came to conquer sin and death, not the Romans. And so it is that the church today holds the belief that Jesus is himself the "Morning Star" of Revelation 22:16, who will come again to rule over His people.

The world today is similar to the world Jesus was born in: we may express it differently in every culture, but part of being human is the longing for a hero, a leader who can show us the way and change everything to good. So many leaders have fallen short of being our needed rescue. So many heroes can only provide temporary good and inspiration. Jesus is the brightest "Star," the one we are waiting for; to settle for less than Jesus we will certainly be disappointed.

SHARE

Read and then discuss the question or questions that are best suited for the age of your child(ren).

1. Turn off the lights, then light and hold up a candle for the whole family to see. Imagine the candle representing Jesus as the promised star we are all waiting for.

2. Brainstorm together a situation where wisdom or guidance is needed by someone in your family this coming year. Look to Jesus as your "star" and let his life point the way. Ask: *what would Jesus who lives in you want you to do?*

3. Pick one person, place, or group that people in our culture turn to for guidance or inspiration when they feel confused, or face difficulties. (For example: social media, political figures, blogs, authors.) Ask: *what kind of advice does this person or group give? How is it helpful and true? How does it fall short of what wisdom Jesus would offer?*

SING
Silent Night

Silent night! Holy night!
All is calm, all is bright
Round yon virgin, mother and child
Holy infant, tender and mild
Sleep in Heavenly peace. (x2)

Silent night! Holy night!
Shepherds quake, at the sight
Glories stream from Heaven above
Heavenly, hosts sing Hallelujah.
Christ the Savior is born. (x2)

PRAY

Thank you, Lord, for knowing our need for wisdom and guidance that this world cannot ever fully offer. Thank you for sending your promised Son, your promised star, to guide us and give us hope for a better tomorrow. Help us see you and follow you in our daily steps into the light of truth.
Amen.

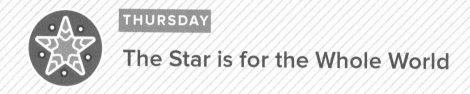
The Star is for the Whole World

FOCUS

The Magi lived far away in a different part of the world from Bethlehem; the star invited them to Jesus. In doing so, the story makes it clear: Jesus came to be a star to guide the whole world to himself. Now, we are to be the light of the world, to help point people to Jesus.

READ

Read about how we are to be salt and light in **Matthew 5:14-16; John 8:12.**

REFLECT

People throughout history have looked up to the stars as their Heavenly guides. Before satellites and even compasses, ship captains and road travelers found their bearings in the sky. The Magi from the East, the shepherds from Bethlehem, and Joseph and Mary from Nazareth all relied on the stars and angels to help guide them. All this points to several enduring truths.

First, everyone needs someone to help them find and know the truth. No one can, without Jesus as their star and light, come home to know God and life as God intended.

Second, when he left this world, Jesus commissioned his disciples to be the smaller stars that point others to the "North star", himself. When Jesus left and filled his followers with his very own Spirit and light, they followed his command to go out in the world. They later planted churches that became "stars" in their own right, extending Jesus' light outward. Their light spread in the first century into the whole Roman Empire; the good news of Jesus has been spreading ever since across the face of our globe.

Not everyone who has seen Jesus' light of truth has believed his message, yet the number of Jesus followers has multiplied exponentially over the centuries. The light of Christ has expanded far and wide from its humble origins in Israel. All regions of the world have been impacted by the good news of Jesus, our promised star.

The church's impact over the centuries was not consistent on each continent. However, in the last decades the good news has reached new regions that are embracing Jesus' light and good news; the center of gravity is shifting from West to East.

There is, however, much work to be done. We live in a time where it seems people from every nation can agree that the challenges are great and truth seems rare. In this time, the church is called to be a "star" that points people to Jesus, who is the brightest star of all.

SHARE

Read and then discuss the question or questions that are best suited for the age of your child(ren).

1. Recall a time and place you and your kids looked up and saw the stars twinkle in the sky, or if the sky is clear, walk outside and look up. Remind yourselves that Jesus made all these stars and the light they bring to the night sky. Can you find the North Star or the Big Dipper? Talk about how people long ago would find their way on land and sea using those same stars as guides.

2. Remember together that many people who love Jesus have traveled to faraway places to be a "star" and to point people to see him. Turn off the lights (optional: shine a light on your tree's star) and pray briefly for a missionary your family knows.

3. Use the internet or your own knowledge to identify an unreached people group somewhere far away. Find their country or region on a map. Take a minute or two to pray for the people and the Jesus followers who may be there.

SING

O Holy Night

O Holy Night! The stars are brightly shining
It is the night of the dear Savior's birth.
Long lay the world in sin and error pining
Till He appeared and the soul felt its worth.
A thrill of hope, the weary world rejoices,
For yonder breaks a new and glorious morn.

Fall on your knees! Oh, hear the angel voices!
O night divine, the night when Christ was born;
O night, O Holy Night, O night divine! (x2)

PRAY

Lord, you came as a star to be seen by the whole world because you love the whole world and the whole world needs you. You have guided us to yourself now by your Spirit, send us out to be your smaller stars and light to a world waiting for hope.
Amen.

We See and Follow God's Star by Faith

FOCUS

The Magi had no certainty about where the star would lead them, nor clarity on what they would find there. They saw and followed by faith, confident that they would somehow be led to a newborn King. We are to see and follow with this same kind of faith in God.

READ

Luke 11:9-13, Hebrews 11:1

REFLECT

The Magi's journey began as a long walk of faith; remember that they could only see and follow the star when it was dark outside. Their God given faith led them to drop everything in order to seek the baby king. There were no tested maps or guarantees. They had an inspired hunch about the star's divine origin, but no specific details about their destination until they arrived at Herod's palace and asked the priests some questions.

Have you ever wondered why only the Magi saw the star and others did not? Undoubtedly, as students of the stars, they kept their eyes riveted up towards the heavens, while everyone else focused on the here and now of earth. Theirs was a life of watching and waiting. When the star rose in the east, they were ready. The Magi saw the star because their faith made them ready to believe what their eyes could not yet fully see.

Seeking and finding is a biblical pattern. When many in the crowd touched Jesus, just one woman received God's power and was healed (Mark 5:29). Why? Because she believed. Her faith led her against all logical conventions to seek out the Rabbi and touch his garment. It was her faith that unlocked his saving touch in her broken body.

Our life, too, is to be marked by seeking and finding. Those of us in the dark who seek Christ by his faith will find Christ through his gift of light.

We are called to join the Magi and the desperate woman, to believe like they did. When we are lost in self-doubt or shame, we can fix on our Bright Star and loving Leader, Jesus Christ, who will never fail us.

SHARE

Read and then discuss the question or questions that are best suited for the age of your child(ren).

1. Have everyone shut their eyes. Ask: *can anyone now see the Christmas tree? No, but do you have faith that it is still there? Yes. Can you see God? No, but you can also believe God is still there.*

2. Blindfold all the family members except the chosen leader, who will represent Jesus. Form a single-file line, putting your hands on the person in front of you. Take a "walk by faith" around the house, trusting your leader won't make you hit a wall or get hurt. Discuss your experience.

3. Clouds, rain, and light pollution hide our ability to see the stars at night, yet we know by "faith" that the stars are still there. Was there for one of you this last year an incident or period of time when God seemed absent, when his presence could not be felt? Ask: *what does your faith tell you about where God was during that incident or period?*

SING

We Three Kings

We three kings of Orient are
Bearing gifts we traverse afar.
Field and fountain, moor and mountain,
Following yonder star.

O star of wonder, star of night,
Star of royal beauty bright,
Westward leading, still proceeding,
Guide us to thy perfect light.

PRAY

Lord Jesus, we believe you are the "star" that can lead us to the truth, and also to see God. Help us step out with your faith when we cannot yet see where the path will lead us, just as the Wise Men did.
Amen.

The Waiting Is Over...Jesus Is Here!

FOCUS

The hundreds of years that Israel waited for the Messiah were over when Jesus was born. We have waited only weeks to celebrate Christ's coming, but our waiting, too, now is over. Jesus has been born. Jesus will come again! It's time to celebrate!

TRADITIONS

- If you wrapped him earlier, unwrap baby Jesus and put him in the Nativity set (or you can wait until Christmas morning before you open your other gifts).

- If you have an Advent wreath with five candles, light the fifth candle (the Christ candle) as well as the other four.

READ

"If He Had Not Come" by Susan E. Murray
It was Christmas Eve—the one night in the year when seven-year-old Bobby was in a hurry to go to bed. His stocking was tacked to the mantel, the beautiful tree stood in the corner. He kissed his mother and father good night and raced upstairs and leaped into bed. It seemed to Bobby that he hadn't been asleep any time when a harsh voice shouted, "Get up!" He opened his eyes, blinking in the bright sunlight. Then he remembered what day it was. With a joyful shout he hurried into his clothes and bounded down the stairs.

On the bottom step he stopped. No stockings hung from the mantel. The Christmas tree was missing. "But...but I put the paper angels on myself," Bobby began as the shrill whistle from the factory nearby made him jump. "The factory can't be open on Christmas!" Bobby thought, as he put on his coat and ran out of the house. The gatekeeper at the factory was his friend. He would tell Bobby why. "Clear out of here, you!" the gatekeeper jerked his thumb at him. "No kids allowed!"

As Bobby slowly turned to go, he saw to his amazement that up and down the street all the stores were open. "Why are they open on Christmas?" he asked a woman coming out of the supermarket. "Christmas?" the woman asked.

"What's that?" The hardware store, the bakery, the five-and-ten—everywhere it was the same. People were busy. They were cross. They'd never heard of Christmas.

"But I know one place where they've heard of Christmas," Bobby cried. "At my church! There's a special service there this morning." He started to run. Here was the street! At least he thought it was, but there was only a weed-filled vacant lot.

The tower with the carillon bells, the Sunday school windows where Bobby had pasted snowflakes—there was nothing there. Just then, from the tall grass near the side of the road, Bobby heard a moan. A man was lying on the ground. "A car struck me," he gasped. "Never even stopped." "Help!" called Bobby to a woman walking past. "This man's hurt." The lady jerked Bobby away. "Don't touch him. He doesn't live here. We don't know anything about him." "I'll run to the hospital, Mister," Bobby promised. "They'll send an ambulance." And he tore off down the street.

Hospital of the Good Samaritan. Bobby had often read the name over the archway in the great stone wall. But now the stone wall ran around an empty field. Where the name of the hospital had been, the following words were carved

instead: If He Had Not Come. Suddenly Bobby was running home as if his life depended on it. Last night his father had read from the Bible. Maybe the Bible would tell him why everything was changed.

The Bible was still lying on the table in the living room. Bobby snatched it up and ran upstairs to his room. But where the New Testament should have started, there were only blank pages. There was no Christmas story—no Jesus at all. Bobby flung himself on his bed and began to cry.

"Merry Christmas, Bobby." It was his mother's voice from downstairs. "Aren't you getting up on Christmas morning?" Bobby sprang out of bed and ran to the window. There was a Christmas wreath on the house across the street. Suddenly the carillon bells from the church tower began to ring, "Joy to the world, the Lord is come!"

"Here I come, Mother," Bobby cried. But he paused at the door and shut his eyes. "You came!" he whispered. "Thank you for coming!"

PRAY

Welcome, Lord Jesus! We are so excited that you came to Earth to be with us, to be our Savior, King, and Friend. And we look forward to your coming again some day! Amen!

Thoughts on Advent and Preparing the Faith of Older Kids

PREPARING KIDS TO LIVE IN A POLARIZED WORLD

I once heard a story of two women immersed in Christmas shopping at a local mall. Tucked in the midst of all the glitter, sale tags, and holiday music, they discovered a small unassuming manger scene. One of the ladies said, "Isn't it just like those Christians to sneak this into Christmas?"

The story reminds me that Christmas brings together two perspectives that are often mutually exclusive. In our family, we wanted to alert our children to this reality, and prepare them for it.

The first view of Christmas I call the *sacred pole*. To those loyal to this perspective, the word "Christmas" means "Christ mass," a worship service for Christ. At Christmas, God's people gather in gratitude to celebrate the coming of Jesus to the world. This good news is remembered in the Bethlehem story. The early Christians established Christmas as a time to remember and share the good news of the loving God who came as a baby and who will one day come as King of Kings.

Supporters of this sacred perspective look to historical evidence to bolster their point. The early church was formally celebrating Christmas by the 4th century. Then came the industrialization of the 19th century and the commercialization of the 20th century, which dramatically added and altered the priorities of the churches previous Christmas celebrations. These new traditions, however, could not change the fact that Christmas for God's people was anchored in the story of Jesus' birth. Many of the most favorite and enduring Christmas symbols originally had their origin in this sacred story, which must be remembered amidst the distorted messaging. People here can hold on to the traditional Christmas carols in church services and radio stations for the true meaning of the holiday.

On the other end of the Christmas spectrum is the *secular pole*. The story of the ladies at the mall illustrates this perspective. It reminds us that many people around the world celebrate this season without reference to the Bethlehem baby.

Advocates of this view can also point to historical evidence to bolster their argument.

Before Christmas was a Christian holiday, the Romans gaily celebrated the winter solstice at this same time of year, anticipating the rebirth of the sun's light into the dark of winter. When Constantine declared Christianity the official religion of the Roman Empire in 327 AD, he also created this sacred holiday, forcing its celebration upon his citizens.

People on this side of the spectrum might also argue that the traditional Christmas symbols don't have any real ties to the original story in the Bible. It's not a religious holiday anymore, they may also say, and shouldn't be treated as such.

It is true that many western Christmas traditions can be traced back to the influence of Charles Dickens' novel, *A Christmas Carol*—not the Bible. The phrase "Merry Christmas," for example, was only first used in a letter to Thomas Cromwell in 1534, centuries after the Bible was completed, and it was Dickens' book that made this phrase so popular today. Furthermore, Dickens' focus on communal meals, family gatherings, generosity, and games filled the vacuum of the 19th century church's otherwise drab and unpopular celebration of Christmas and became how most of us pass the days around December 25th.

Endearing and non-sacred symbols have emerged from the secular pole as well. Holiday traditions and songs that have no reference to Christ abound in countries all over the world.

Instead, these traditions celebrate the values of family, love, and generosity—or simply celebrate the winter season of snow and sleigh bells, a fireside glow and feelings of happiness. Some even assert that the Christmas tree can be traced back to pagan festivals.

Putting up lights, shopping for gifts, wrapping and opening presents, filling stockings, decorating, attending gatherings with family and friends and parties at work, eating good food, baking for neighbors, and even buying a present for a needy child—these symbolic activities do not originate from, nor even require a belief in, the Bethlehem story. Rather, those of this secular pole might argue, these practices are cultural traditions that meet our human need to celebrate and offer a needed reprieve from winter's dreariness.

Where do these polarized perspectives lead those of us who follow Jesus and want to faithfully celebrate Christmas? How do we live as a light in this season in a world fraught with darkness?

THE TENSION BETWEEN SACRED AND SECULAR

Many of us intuitively know that this polarization of sacred and secular is artificial. This unnecessary dichotomy produces alienation between the church and the unreligious. Like other poles found in politics, economics, and religion, taking an extreme perspective often leaves us unnecessarily angry or alienated. Most importantly, the sacred and secular poles debate distracts us from a wiser way forward.

Some dramatically oppose the secular pole of Christmas and want nothing to do with its distracting impurities and perversions. Others are more comfortable only going to church Christmas Eve and celebrating the rest of the season along with the secular pole. However, many of us dislike this split; we don't want to fall into the "either/or" way of living or celebrating Christmas. We can sense there must be a middle road.

Christmas, like the rest of life, is not simply light or dark, black or white. Both poles of the attitude toward Christmas contain truth and must somehow be embraced together. Celebrating Christmas "between the poles" helps us recognize that this holiday's origins are mixed. They are both sacred and secular.

Our goal during Christmas is to let both the sacred and secular sides coexist together in tension, but not because both are equally true. Rather, it is the nature of the church to be in the world, but not of it. Our homes during Advent should be like a greenhouse, a safe place where we can practice living like Christ in the world. The practice of understanding what matters to the world, finding the inherent truth within it, and then pointing others to Christ in word and deed is an art that this new generation of believers must master. We must do so for the sake of the world and for the sake of our own faith.

AND CHRISTMAS IS A PERFECT TIME TO PRACTICE THIS.

So, in this Advent book, sacred and secular symbols are embraced equally with no judgment made, and are all presented as a conduit to see Jesus. Sometimes we see Christ directly in the symbols, like the Nativity, the angels, and the star. Sometimes the Christmas message is indirect, like in the ornaments, gifts, candy canes, and lights. When our families discover Christ's story and truth in the Christmas symbols, we will be better able to see Christ more often in our daily lives, and even in the harder places of commercials and billboards, marketplaces and movies, playgrounds and parties, courthouses and college campuses.

This has been my hope as we raised our children. Now it is the hope of this book.

Guideposts Christmas Treasury Readings

The New Guideposts Christmas Treasury (Minneapolis: Fortress Press, 1989)

WEEK 1

- Sunday: "A Long Way Home," pp. 89-94 (A family Christmas story about a tree and candles from WWII).
- Monday: "A Christmas Garden," p. 84 (A short prayer).
- Tuesday: "Christmas is a Time for Imagination," pp. 88-89 (Prisoners make a tree, then darkness comes). See also the story on pp. 98-99.
- Wednesday: "My Evergreen Memory," pp. 169-172 (A tree is given to a poor immigrant family).
- Thursday: "The Caring Tree," pp. 159-162 (A story of the change a church can bring).
- Friday: "Lord, Watch Over These Your Special Children," pp. 71-74 (A special needs choir on tour reaches out to the lost).
- Saturday: "I Remember Three Christmases III," pp. 99-100 (The hope we have even when death comes on Christmas).

WEEK 2

- Sunday: "Davie's Gift," pp. 67-69 (A special and unique manger lights up an otherwise dark Christmas).
- Monday: "Undelivered Gifts," pp. 210-211 (Some soldiers make the love of God visible and a baby is born).
- Tuesday: "At Christmas the Heart Goes Home," pp. 37-40 (A picture of Heaven as loved ones re-gather).
- Wednesday: "Trouble at the Inn," pp. 75-76 (The innkeeper ad libs and makes a Christmas pageant unforgettable).
- Thursday: "Sincerely," pp. 85-86 (The power of memories of a special ornament from childhood).

- Friday: "Bittersweet Christmas," pp. 104-105 (Four Jewish women make a Christmas tree possible).
- Saturday: "Surprise Ending," pp. 212-214 (Love's magic happens as one family reaches out to another poor family).

WEEK 3

- Sunday: "The Christmas I Remember Best," pp. 86-87 (The gift of God's love is the heart of Christmas). See also the prayer on p. 166 and a family tradition idea on pp. 20-21.
- Monday: "The Gift of Sharing," pp. 52-53 (A stranger leaves a small and surprising gift). See also the poem on p. 197.
- Tuesday: "Pattern of Love," pp. 64-65 (Two boys and a shopkeeper sacrifice to buy the boys' dad a special gift).
- Wednesday: "Blessings in Disguise," pp. 175-177 (Christmas gifts that did not meet expectations).
- Thursday: "A Gift of the Heart," pp. 187-190 (A visitor comes like Santa in New York.) See also the story on pp. 24-27.
- Friday: "Because of a Baby," pp. 155-159 (Everyone in the apartment shares with the new strangers in need). See also the ideas for creative gifts on pp. 148-150.
- Saturday: "The Night of the Blizzard," pp. 151-155 (A church says "yes" when a blizzard comes). See also "Trouble at Wallen Creek," pp. 101-104 (Two unlikely men say "yes" and change everything).

WEEK 4

- Sunday: "Waiting, Waiting for Christmas," pp. 57-59 (God speaks a Christmas Eve miracle).
- Monday: "Just One Small Candle," pp. 201-202 (An extinguished candle leads to a miracle for a young boy).
- Tuesday: "The Star and the Cross are always there," p. 70 (A widow needs help to see the truth).
- Wednesday: "The Empty Room," pp. 31-33 (God leads a mourning woman to see differently).
- Thursday: "I Remember Three Christmases II," pp. 98-99 (A final prayer with a "sinful" woman on her death bed at Christmas).

Memories and Traditions

1. Where did we celebrate Christmas Eve and day this year, and who joined us?

2. What activities, gatherings and events during the season did we do?

3. What traditions did we do (this book and otherwise)?

4. Was there a special present(s) given?

5. Anything else we want to remember?

Our Christmas Celebration 20____

Memories and Traditions

1. Where did we celebrate Christmas Eve and day this year, and who joined us?

2. What activities, gatherings and events during the season did we do?

3. What traditions did we do (this book and otherwise)?

4. Was there a special present(s) given?

5. Anything else we want to remember?

Memories and Traditions

1. Where did we celebrate Christmas Eve and day this year, and who joined us?

_____

_____

_____

2. What activities, gatherings and events during the season did we do?

_____

_____

_____

3. What traditions did we do (this book and otherwise)?

_____

_____

4. Was there a special present(s) given?

_____

_____

5. Anything else we want to remember?

_____

_____

Our Christmas Celebration 20_____

Memories and Traditions

1. Where did we celebrate Christmas Eve and day this year, and who joined us?

2. What activities, gatherings and events during the season did we do?

3. What traditions did we do (this book and otherwise)?

4. Was there a special present(s) given?

5. Anything else we want to remember?

Our Christmas Celebration   20_____

Memories and Traditions

1. Where did we celebrate Christmas Eve and day this year, and who joined us?

2. What activities, gatherings and events during the season did we do?

3. What traditions did we do (this book and otherwise)?

4. Was there a special present(s) given?

5. Anything else we want to remember?

Our Christmas Celebration 20____

Memories and Traditions

1. Where did we celebrate Christmas Eve and day this year, and who joined us?

2. What activities, gatherings and events during the season did we do?

3. What traditions did we do (this book and otherwise)?

4. Was there a special present(s) given?

5. Anything else we want to remember?

Our Christmas Celebration 20____

Memories and Traditions

1. Where did we celebrate Christmas Eve and day this year, and who joined us?

2. What activities, gatherings and events during the season did we do?

3. What traditions did we do (this book and otherwise)?

4. Was there a special present(s) given?

5. Anything else we want to remember?

Our Christmas Celebration   20____

Memories and Traditions

1. Where did we celebrate Christmas Eve and day this year, and who joined us?

2. What activities, gatherings and events during the season did we do?

3. What traditions did we do (this book and otherwise)?

4. Was there a special present(s) given?

5. Anything else we want to remember?

Memories and Traditions

1. Where did we celebrate Christmas Eve and day this year, and who joined us?

2. What activities, gatherings and events during the season did we do?

3. What traditions did we do (this book and otherwise)?

4. Was there a special present(s) given?

5. Anything else we want to remember?

Our Christmas Celebration 20____

Memories and Traditions

1. Where did we celebrate Christmas Eve and day this year, and who joined us?

2. What activities, gatherings and events during the season did we do?

3. What traditions did we do (this book and otherwise)?

4. Was there a special present(s) given?

5. Anything else we want to remember?

Our Christmas Celebration   20____

Memories and Traditions

1. Where did we celebrate Christmas Eve and day this year, and who joined us?

_____

_____

_____

2. What activities, gatherings and events during the season did we do?

_____

_____

_____

3. What traditions did we do (this book and otherwise)?

_____

_____

4. Was there a special present(s) given?

_____

_____

5. Anything else we want to remember?

_____

_____

Our Christmas Celebration 20_____

Memories and Traditions

1. Where did we celebrate Christmas Eve and day this year, and who joined us?

2. What activities, gatherings and events during the season did we do?

3. What traditions did we do (this book and otherwise)?

4. Was there a special present(s) given?

5. Anything else we want to remember?

Memories and Traditions

1. Where did we celebrate Christmas Eve and day this year, and who joined us?

2. What activities, gatherings and events during the season did we do?

3. What traditions did we do (this book and otherwise)?

4. Was there a special present(s) given?

5. Anything else we want to remember?

Our Christmas Celebration   20_____

Memories and Traditions

1. Where did we celebrate Christmas Eve and day this year, and who joined us?

2. What activities, gatherings and events during the season did we do?

3. What traditions did we do (this book and otherwise)?

4. Was there a special present(s) given?

5. Anything else we want to remember?

Memories and Traditions

1. Where did we celebrate Christmas Eve and day this year, and who joined us?

2. What activities, gatherings and events during the season did we do?

3. What traditions did we do (this book and otherwise)?

4. Was there a special present(s) given?

5. Anything else we want to remember?

Our Christmas Celebration 20____

Memories and Traditions

1. Where did we celebrate Christmas Eve and day this year, and who joined us?

2. What activities, gatherings and events during the season did we do?

3. What traditions did we do (this book and otherwise)?

4. Was there a special present(s) given?

5. Anything else we want to remember?

Our Christmas Celebration   20_____

Memories and Traditions

1. Where did we celebrate Christmas Eve and day this year, and who joined us?

2. What activities, gatherings and events during the season did we do?

3. What traditions did we do (this book and otherwise)?

4. Was there a special present(s) given?

5. Anything else we want to remember?

Our Christmas Celebration   20____

Memories and Traditions

1. Where did we celebrate Christmas Eve and day this year, and who joined us?

2. What activities, gatherings and events during the season did we do?

3. What traditions did we do (this book and otherwise)?

4. Was there a special present(s) given?

5. Anything else we want to remember?

Memories and Traditions

1. Where did we celebrate Christmas Eve and day this year, and who joined us?

2. What activities, gatherings and events during the season did we do?

3. What traditions did we do (this book and otherwise)?

4. Was there a special present(s) given?

5. Anything else we want to remember?

Our Christmas Celebration   20____

Memories and Traditions

1. Where did we celebrate Christmas Eve and day this year, and who joined us?

2. What activities, gatherings and events during the season did we do?

3. What traditions did we do (this book and otherwise)?

4. Was there a special present(s) given?

5. Anything else we want to remember?

CPSIA information can be obtained
at www.ICGtesting.com
Printed in the USA
LVHW071602191122
733598LV00020B/1357